Holiday Fun

Recipes to make your own gifts

Use these recipes to delight your friends and family. Each recipe includes gift tags for your convenience — just cut them out and personalize!

To decorate jars, cut fabric in 9" diameter circles. Screw down the jar ring to hold fabric in place or hold fabric with a ribbon, raffia, twine, yarn, lace or string (first secure the fabric with a rubber band before tying). Punch a hole into the corner of the tag and use the ribbon, raffia, twine, yarn, lace or string to attach the tag to the jar.

These gifts should keep for up to six months. If the mix contains nuts, it should be used within three months.

Printed in the United States of America
by G&R Publishing Co.

Distributed By:

507 Industrial Street
Waverly, IA 50677

ISBN 1-56383-137-6
Item #3008

Oatmeal Fruit Cookie Mix

3 T. sugar

1/2 C. plus 1 T. wheat germ

1/3 C. dried cherries or
cranberries

1/3 C. raisins

1/2 C. flaked coconut

1/3 C. brown sugar

3/4 C. quick cooking oats

3/4 C. flour

1/4 tsp. plus 1/8 tsp. baking
soda

1/4 tsp. plus 1/8 tsp. salt

Layer the ingredients in the order given into a wide-mouth 1-quart canning jar. Pack each layer into place before adding the next ingredient.

Attach a gift tag with the mixing and baking directions.

Oatmeal Fruit Cookies

1 jar Oatmeal Fruit Cookie Mix
6 T. butter or margarine,
   softened
1 egg
3/4 tsp. vanilla
3 T. milk

Preheat the oven to 350°F. In a medium bowl, cream the butter, egg, vanilla and milk. Add the Oatmeal Fruit Cookie Mix and stir until well blended. Shape into 1-inch balls. Place on a greased baking sheet. Bake for 10 to 14 minutes or until cookies are a light golden brown. Transfer to wire racks to cool.

Oatmeal Fruit Cookies

1 jar Oatmeal Fruit Cookie Mix
6 T. butter or margarine,
  softened

1 egg
3/4 tsp. vanilla
3 T. milk

    Preheat the oven to 350°F. In a medium bowl, cream the butter, egg, vanilla and milk. Add the Oatmeal Fruit Cookie Mix and stir until well blended. Shape into 1-inch balls. Place on a greased baking sheet. Bake for 10 to 14 minutes or until cookies are a light golden brown. Transfer to wire racks to cool.

Oatmeal Fruit Cookies

1 jar Oatmeal Fruit Cookie Mix
6 T. butter or margarine,
  softened

1 egg
3/4 tsp. vanilla
3 T. milk

    Preheat the oven to 350°F. In a medium bowl, cream the butter, egg, vanilla and milk. Add the Oatmeal Fruit Cookie Mix and stir until well blended. Shape into 1-inch balls. Place on a greased baking sheet. Bake for 10 to 14 minutes or until cookies are a light golden brown. Transfer to wire racks to cool.

Oatmeal Fruit Cookies

1 jar Oatmeal Fruit Cookie Mix
6 T. butter or margarine,
  softened

1 egg
3/4 tsp. vanilla
3 T. milk

    Preheat the oven to 350°F. In a medium bowl, cream the butter, egg, vanilla and milk. Add the Oatmeal Fruit Cookie Mix and stir until well blended. Shape into 1-inch balls. Place on a greased baking sheet. Bake for 10 to 14 minutes or until cookies are a light golden brown. Transfer to wire racks to cool.

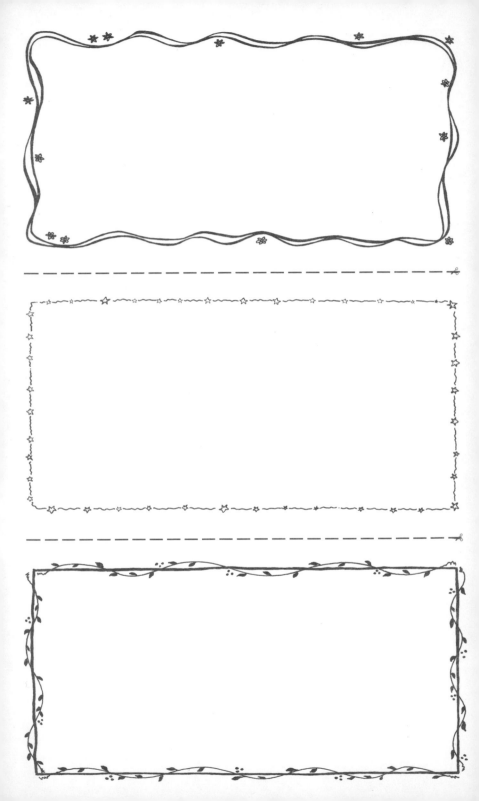

Oatmeal Fruit Cookies

1 jar Oatmeal Fruit Cookie Mix
6 T. butter or margarine,
   softened

1 egg
3/4 tsp. vanilla
3 T. milk

Preheat the oven to 350°F. In a medium bowl, cream the butter, egg, vanilla and milk. Add the Oatmeal Fruit Cookie Mix and stir until well blended. Shape into 1-inch balls. Place on a greased baking sheet. Bake for 10 to 14 minutes or until cookies are a light golden brown. Transfer to wire racks to cool.

Oatmeal Fruit Cookies

1 Jar Oatmeal Fruit Cookie Mix
6 T. butter or margarine,
   softened

1 egg
3/4 tsp. vanilla
3 T. milk

Preheat the oven to 350°F. In a medium bowl, cream the butter, egg, vanilla and milk. Add the Oatmeal Fruit Cookie Mix and stir until well blended. Shape into 1-inch balls. Place on a greased baking sheet. Bake for 10 to 14 minutes or until cookies are a light golden brown. Transfer to wire racks to cool.

Oatmeal Fruit Cookies

1 jar Oatmeal Fruit Cookie Mix
6 T. butter or margarine,
   softened

1 egg
3/4 tsp. vanilla
3 T. milk

Preheat the oven to 350°F. In a medium bowl, cream the butter, egg, vanilla and milk. Add the Oatmeal Fruit Cookie Mix and stir until well blended. Shape into 1-inch balls. Place on a greased baking sheet. Bake for 10 to 14 minutes or until cookies are a light golden brown. Transfer to wire racks to cool.

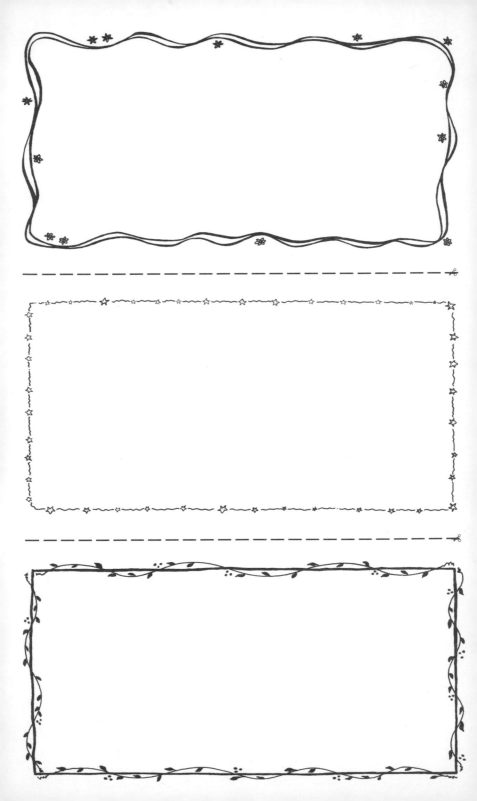

Spice-n-Ginger Cookie Mix

1 C. sugar
1/4 tsp. plus 1/8 tsp. salt
1/2 tsp. plus 1/8 tsp. baking
   soda
3/4 tsp. ginger
1 1/4 tsp. cinnamon
1 1/4 tsp. ground cloves
3 1/3 C. all-purpose flour

Layer the ingredients in the order given into a wide-mouth 1-quart canning jar. Pack each layer into place before adding the next ingredient.

Attach a gift tag with the mixing and baking directions.

❀ *A half-yard of fabric should make eight wide-mouth jar covers.* ❀

Spice-n-Ginger Cookies

1 jar Spice-n-Ginger Cookie Mix
1/2 C. plus 1/3 C. (13 T.) butter
   or margarine, softened
5 T. molasses
2 eggs
3/4 tsp. vanilla

Preheat the oven to 350°F. In a large bowl, cream butter until light and fluffy. Add molasses, eggs and vanilla and beat until mixed well. Stir in the Spice-n-Ginger Cookie Mix until well combined. Drop dough by teaspoonfuls on a greased cookie sheet. Bake for 12 to 14 minutes. Transfer to wire racks to cool.

Spice-n-Ginger Cookies

1 jar Spice-n-Ginger Cookie Mix   5 T. molasses
1/2 C. plus 1/3 C. (13 T.) butter   2 eggs
   or margarine, softened   3/4 tsp. vanilla

   Preheat the oven to 350°F. In a large bowl, cream butter until light and fluffy. Add molasses, eggs and vanilla and beat until mixed well. Stir in the Spice-n-Ginger Cookie Mix until well combined. Drop dough by teaspoonfuls on a greased cookie sheet. Bake for 12 to 14 minutes. Transfer to wire racks to cool.

Spice-n-Ginger Cookies

1 jar Spice-n-Ginger Cookie Mix   5 T. molasses
1/2 C. plus 1/3 C. (13 T.) butter   2 eggs
   or margarine, softened   3/4 tsp. vanilla

   Preheat the oven to 350°F. In a large bowl, cream butter until light and fluffy. Add molasses, eggs and vanilla and beat until mixed well. Stir in the Spice-n-Ginger Cookie Mix until well combined. Drop dough by teaspoonfuls on a greased cookie sheet. Bake for 12 to 14 minutes. Transfer to wire racks to cool.

Spice-n-Ginger Cookies

1 jar Spice-n-Ginger Cookie Mix   5 T. molasses
1/2 C. plus 1/3 C. (13 T.) butter   2 eggs
   or margarine, softened   3/4 tsp. vanilla

   Preheat the oven to 350°F. In a large bowl, cream butter until light and fluffy. Add molasses, eggs and vanilla and beat until mixed well. Stir in the Spice-n-Ginger Cookie Mix until well combined. Drop dough by teaspoonfuls on a greased cookie sheet. Bake for 12 to 14 minutes. Transfer to wire racks to cool.

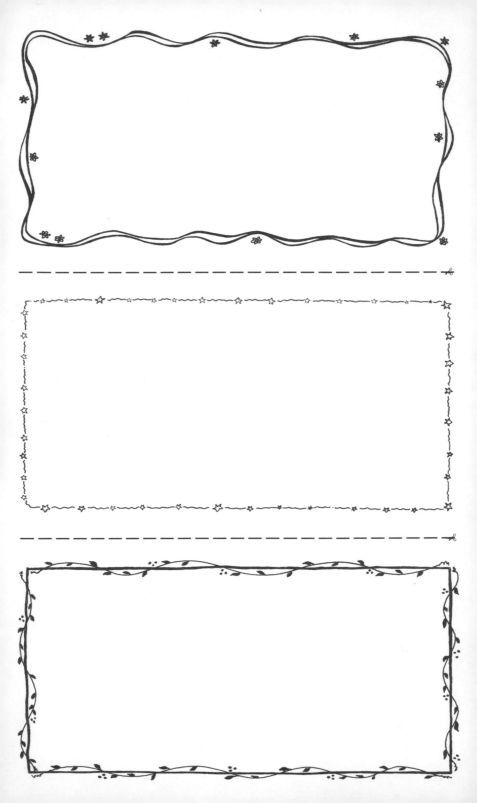

Spice-n-Ginger Cookies

1 jar Spice-n-Ginger Cookie Mix   5 T. molasses
1/2 C. plus 1/3 C. (13 T.) butter   2 eggs
   or margarine, softened   3/4 tsp. vanilla

    Preheat the oven to 350°F. In a large bowl, cream butter until light and fluffy. Add molasses, eggs and vanilla and beat until mixed well. Stir in the Spice-n-Ginger Cookie Mix until well combined. Drop dough by teaspoonfuls on a greased cookie sheet. Bake for 12 to 14 minutes. Transfer to wire racks to cool.

Spice-n-Ginger Cookies

1 jar Spice-n-Ginger Cookie Mix   5 T. molasses
1/2 C. plus 1/3 C. (13 T.) butter   2 eggs
   or margarine, softened   3/4 tsp. vanilla

    Preheat the oven to 350°F. In a large bowl, cream butter until light and fluffy. Add molasses, eggs and vanilla and beat until mixed well. Stir in the Spice-n-Ginger Cookie Mix until well combined. Drop dough by teaspoonfuls on a greased cookie sheet. Bake for 12 to 14 minutes. Transfer to wire racks to cool.

Spice-n-Ginger Cookies

1 jar Spice-n-Ginger Cookie Mix   5 T. molasses
1/2 C. plus 1/3 C. (13 T.) butter   2 eggs
   or margarine, softened   3/4 tsp. vanilla

    Preheat the oven to 350°F. In a large bowl, cream butter until light and fluffy. Add molasses, eggs and vanilla and beat until mixed well. Stir in the Spice-n-Ginger Cookie Mix until well combined. Drop dough by teaspoonfuls on a greased cookie sheet. Bake for 12 to 14 minutes. Transfer to wire racks to cool.

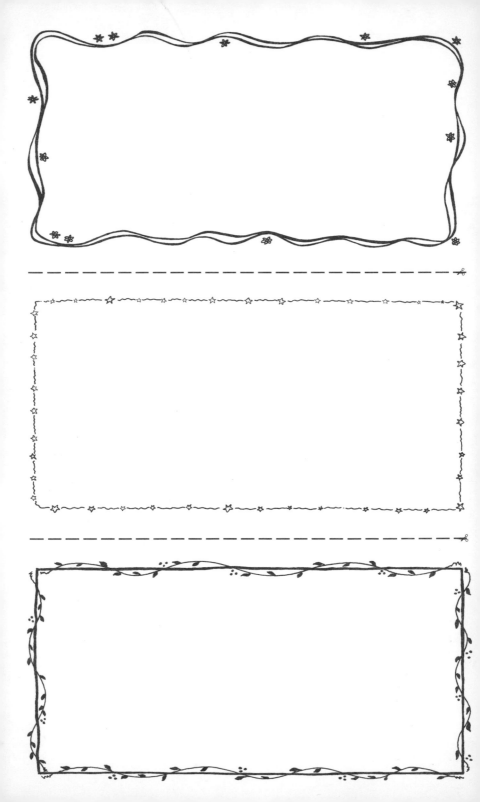

Santa's Bounty Cookie Mix

1/4 C. sugar
3/4 C. wheat germ
1 C. quick oats
2/3 C. flaked coconut
1/2 C. dried cherries
1/2 C. raisins
1/2 C. brown sugar
1 C. all-purpose flour
1/2 tsp. baking soda
1/2 tsp. salt

Layer the ingredients in the order given into a wide-mouth 1-quart canning jar. Pack each layer into place before adding the next ingredient.

Attach a gift tag with the mixing and baking directions.

Santa's Bounty Cookies

Makes 2 dozen

1 jar Santa's Bounty Cookie Mix
1/2 C. butter or margarine,
   softened
1 egg
1 tsp. vanilla
1/4 C. milk

Preheat the oven to 350°F. In a large bowl, place Santa's Bounty Cookie Mix and stir. Work in butter until the mixture resembles coarse crumbs. Add egg, vanilla and milk and stir until the mixture is well blended. Drop teaspoonfuls 2 inches apart on a greased cookie sheet. Bake for 10 to 14 minutes or until the edges are lightly browned. Transfer to wire racks to cool.

Santa's Bounty Cookies
Makes 2 dozen

1 jar Santa's Bounty Cookie Mix
1/2 C. butter or margarine,
  softened

1 egg
1 tsp. vanilla
1/4 C. milk

Preheat the oven to 350°F. In a large bowl, place Santa's Bounty Cookie Mix and stir. Work in butter until the mixture resembles coarse crumbs. Add egg, vanilla and milk and stir until the mixture is well blended. Drop teaspoonfuls 2 inches apart on a greased cookie sheet. Bake for 10 to 14 minutes or until the edges are lightly browned. Transfer to wire racks to cool.

Santa's Bounty Cookies
Makes 2 dozen

1 jar Santa's Bounty Cookie Mix
1/2 C. butter or margarine,
  softened

1 egg
1 tsp. vanilla
1/4 C. milk

Preheat the oven to 350°F. In a large bowl, place Santa's Bounty Cookie Mix and stir. Work in butter until the mixture resembles coarse crumbs. Add egg, vanilla and milk and stir until the mixture is well blended. Drop teaspoonfuls 2 inches apart on a greased cookie sheet. Bake for 10 to 14 minutes or until the edges are lightly browned. Transfer to wire racks to cool.

Santa's Bounty Cookies
Makes 2 dozen

1 jar Santa's Bounty Cookie Mix
1/2 C. butter or margarine,
  softened

1 egg
1 tsp. vanilla
1/4 C. milk

Preheat the oven to 350°F. In a large bowl, place Santa's Bounty Cookie Mix and stir. Work in butter until the mixture resembles coarse crumbs. Add egg, vanilla and milk and stir until the mixture is well blended. Drop teaspoonfuls 2 inches apart on a greased cookie sheet. Bake for 10 to 14 minutes or until the edges are lightly browned. Transfer to wire racks to cool.

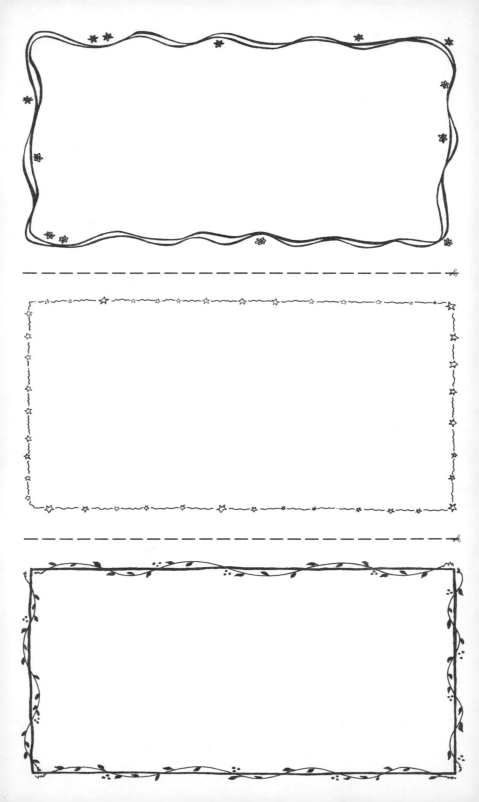

Santa's Bounty Cookies
Makes 2 dozen

1 jar Santa's Bounty Cookie Mix
1/2 C. butter or margarine,
  softened

1 egg
1 tsp. vanilla
1/4 C. milk

    Preheat the oven to 350°F. In a large bowl, place Santa's Bounty Cookie Mix and stir. Work in butter until the mixture resembles coarse crumbs. Add egg, vanilla and milk and stir until the mixture is well blended. Drop teaspoonfuls 2 inches apart on a greased cookie sheet. Bake for 10 to 14 minutes or until the edges are lightly browned. Transfer to wire racks to cool.

Santa's Bounty Cookies
Makes 2 dozen

1 jar Santa's Bounty Cookie Mix
1/2 C. butter or margarine,
  softened

1 egg
1 tsp. vanilla
1/4 C. milk

    Preheat the oven to 350°F. In a large bowl, place Santa's Bounty Cookie Mix and stir. Work in butter until the mixture resembles coarse crumbs. Add egg, vanilla and milk and stir until the mixture is well blended. Drop teaspoonfuls 2 inches apart on a greased cookie sheet. Bake for 10 to 14 minutes or until the edges are lightly browned. Transfer to wire racks to cool.

Santa's Bounty Cookies
Makes 2 dozen

1 jar Santa's Bounty Cookie Mix
1/2 C. butter or margarine,
  softened

1 egg
1 tsp. vanilla
1/4 C. milk

    Preheat the oven to 350°F. In a large bowl, place Santa's Bounty Cookie Mix and stir. Work in butter until the mixture resembles coarse crumbs. Add egg, vanilla and milk and stir until the mixture is well blended. Drop teaspoonfuls 2 inches apart on a greased cookie sheet. Bake for 10 to 14 minutes or until the edges are lightly browned. Transfer to wire racks to cool.

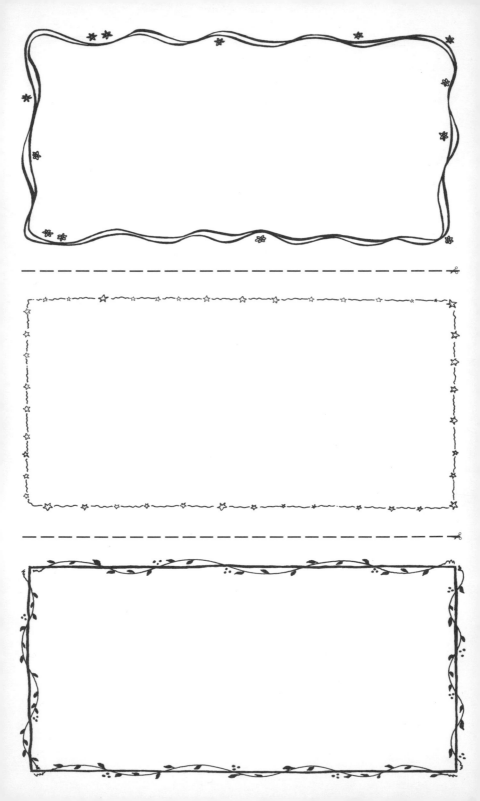

Mocha Rum Ball Mix

2 C. crushed vanilla wafers
1 1/2 C. powdered sugar
1 C. almonds, finely chopped
2 T. unsweetened cocoa
1 1/2 tsp. instant coffee
   granules
1/2 tsp. cinnamon, optional

Layer the ingredients in the order given into a wide-mouth 1-quart canning jar. Pack each layer into place before adding the next ingredient.

Attach a gift tag with the mixing directions.

For a different look, place a small amount of stuffing under a fabric cover before attaching to "puff" the top.

Mocha Rum Balls

1 jar Mocha Rum Ball Mix
4 T. rum
4 T. coffee
1/4 C. powdered sugar

In a large bowl, place Mocha Rum Ball Mix. Add rum and coffee. Stir the mixture until well blended. Form into small balls. Roll the balls in powdered sugar. Place on a cookie sheet to dry. Store in an airtight container.

Mocha Rum Balls

1 jar Mocha Rum Ball Mix   4 T. coffee
4 T. rum   1/4 C. powdered sugar

    In a large bowl, place Mocha Rum Ball Mix. Add rum and coffee. Stir the mixture until well blended. Form into small balls. Roll the balls in powdered sugar. Place on a cookie sheet to dry. Store in an airtight container.

Mocha Rum Balls

1 jar Mocha Rum Ball Mix   4 T. coffee
4 T. rum   1/4 C. powdered sugar

    In a large bowl, place Mocha Rum Ball Mix. Add rum and coffee. Stir the mixture until well blended. Form into small balls. Roll the balls in powdered sugar. Place on a cookie sheet to dry. Store in an airtight container.

Mocha Rum Balls

1 jar Mocha Rum Ball Mix   4 T. coffee
4 T. rum   1/4 C. powdered sugar

    In a large bowl, place Mocha Rum Ball Mix. Add rum and coffee. Stir the mixture until well blended. Form into small balls. Roll the balls in powdered sugar. Place on a cookie sheet to dry. Store in an airtight container.

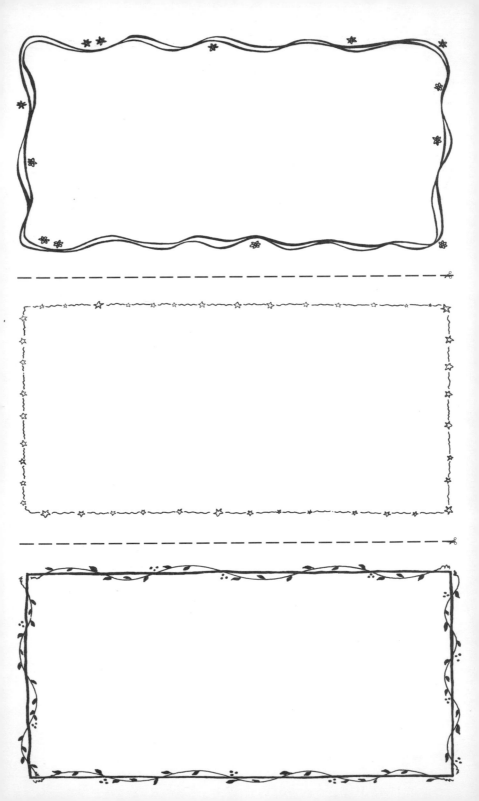

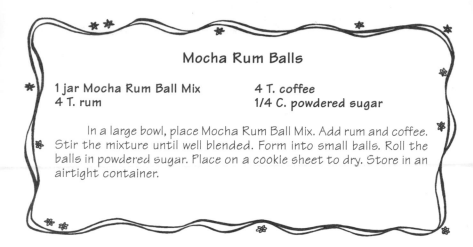

Mocha Rum Balls

1 jar Mocha Rum Ball Mix   4 T. coffee
4 T. rum   1/4 C. powdered sugar

    In a large bowl, place Mocha Rum Ball Mix. Add rum and coffee. Stir the mixture until well blended. Form into small balls. Roll the balls in powdered sugar. Place on a cookie sheet to dry. Store in an airtight container.

Mocha Rum Balls

1 jar Mocha Rum Ball Mix   4 T. coffee
4 T. rum   1/4 C. powdered sugar

    In a large bowl, place Mocha Rum Ball Mix. Add rum and coffee. Stir the mixture until well blended. Form into small balls. Roll the balls in powdered sugar. Place on a cookie sheet to dry. Store in an airtight container.

Mocha Rum Balls

1 jar Mocha Rum Ball Mix   4 T. coffee
4 T. rum   1/4 C. powdered sugar

    In a large bowl, place Mocha Rum Ball Mix. Add rum and coffee. Stir the mixture until well blended. Form into small balls. Roll the balls in powdered sugar. Place on a cookie sheet to dry. Store in an airtight container.

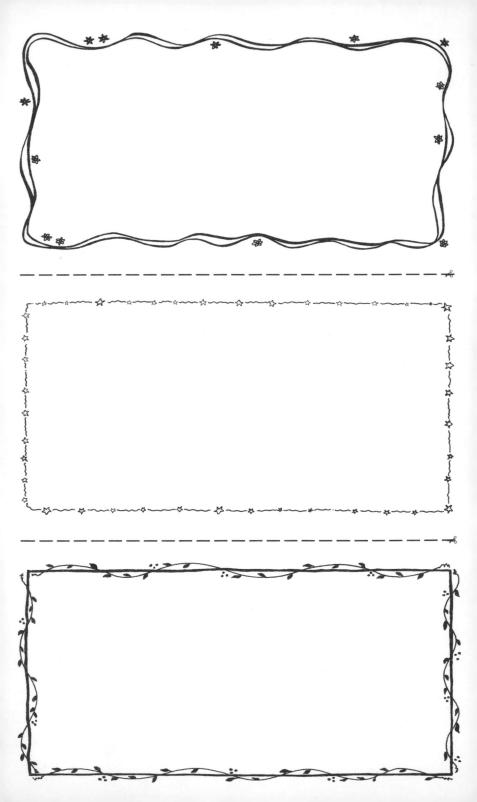

Spice Cake Mix

1 1/2 C. whole wheat flour
3/4 C. sugar
1/3 C. chopped nuts
1/2 C. raisins
1/2 C. plus 1 T. brown sugar
1/4 C. powdered instant dry milk
3/4 tsp. salt
1 tsp. baking powder
3/4 tsp. baking soda
3/4 tsp. cinnamon
1/4 tsp. plus 1/8 tsp. nutmeg
1/4 tsp. plus 1/8 tsp. ground
   cloves

Layer the ingredients in the order given into a wide-mouth 1-quart canning jar. Pack each layer into place before adding the next ingredient.

Attach a gift tag with the mixing and baking directions.

Spice Cake

1 jar Spice Cake Mix
1 1/2 C. applesauce
2 eggs

Preheat the oven to 325°F. In a large bowl, mix the applesauce and eggs. Add the Spice Cake Mix and stir until the mixture is well blended. Spread batter into a well greased tube pan. Bake for 45 to 55 minutes. Cool in the pan on a wire rack before removing.

Spice Cake

1 jar Spice Cake Mix   **2 eggs**
1 1/2 C. applesauce

Preheat the oven to 325°F. In a large bowl, mix the applesauce and eggs. Add the Spice Cake Mix and stir until the mixture is well blended. Spread batter into a well greased tube pan. Bake for 45 to 55 minutes. Cool in the pan on a wire rack before removing.

Spice Cake

1 jar Spice Cake Mix   **2 eggs**
1 1/2 C. applesauce

Preheat the oven to 325°F. In a large bowl, mix the applesauce and eggs. Add the Spice Cake Mix and stir until the mixture is well blended. Spread batter into a well greased tube pan. Bake for 45 to 55 minutes. Cool in the pan on a wire rack before removing.

Spice Cake

1 jar Spice Cake Mix   **2 eggs**
1 1/2 C. applesauce

Preheat the oven to 325°F. In a large bowl, mix the applesauce and eggs. Add the Spice Cake Mix and stir until the mixture is well blended. Spread batter into a well greased tube pan. Bake for 45 to 55 minutes. Cool in the pan on a wire rack before removing.

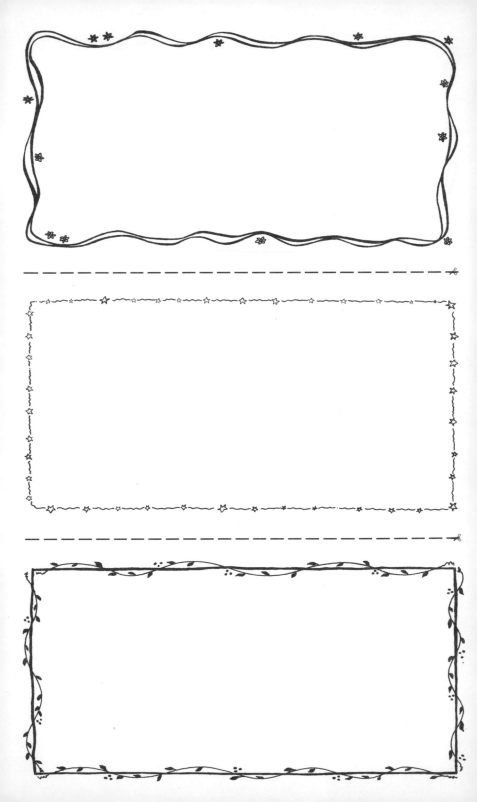

Spice Cake

1 jar Spice Cake Mix **2 eggs**
1 1/2 C. applesauce

Preheat the oven to 325°F. In a large bowl, mix the applesauce and eggs. Add the Spice Cake Mix and stir until the mixture is well blended. Spread batter into a well greased tube pan. Bake for 45 to 55 minutes. Cool in the pan on a wire rack before removing.

Spice Cake

1 jar Spice Cake Mix **2 eggs**
1 1/2 C. applesauce

Preheat the oven to 325°F. In a large bowl, mix the applesauce and eggs. Add the Spice Cake Mix and stir until the mixture is well blended. Spread batter into a well greased tube pan. Bake for 45 to 55 minutes. Cool in the pan on a wire rack before removing.

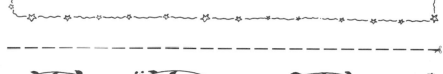

Spice Cake

1 jar Spice Cake Mix **2 eggs**
1 1/2 C. applesauce

Preheat the oven to 325°F. In a large bowl, mix the applesauce and eggs. Add the Spice Cake Mix and stir until the mixture is well blended. Spread batter into a well greased tube pan. Bake for 45 to 55 minutes. Cool in the pan on a wire rack before removing.

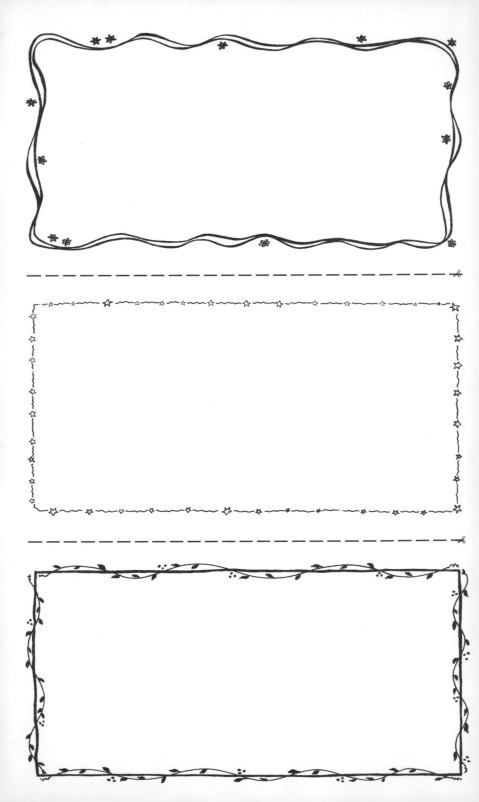

Holiday Bean Soup Mix

1/2 C. dry kidney beans
1/2 C. split green peas
1/2 C. dry black beans
1/2 C. red lentils
1/2 C. dry red beans
1/2 C. split green peas

Seasoning Packet:

1 T. dried green pepper flakes
2 tsp. chicken bouillon granules
2 tsp. dried minced onion
1 1/2 tsp. salt
1/2 tsp. dried parsley flakes
1/2 tsp. pepper
1/2 tsp. garlic powder
1/2 tsp. celery seed
4 T. brown sugar

Layer the ingredients in the order given into a wide-mouth 1-quart canning jar. Mix and place the seasonings in a small plastic bag. Place the packet on top of the peas.

Attach a gift tag with the cooking directions.

Holiday Bean Soup

Makes about 5 servings

1 jar Holiday Bean Soup Mix
2 cans (14 1/2 oz. each)
stewed tomatoes
1 tsp. liquid smoke (optional)

Remove seasoning bag from Holiday Bean Soup Mix and set aside. Rinse beans and place in a large soup pot. Pour 4 cups boiling water over beans, cover and let soak overnight. Drain water. Add 6 cups water. Cover and bring to a boil over high heat, stirring occasionally. Reduce heat to low and simmer 1 to 1 1/2 hours or until beans are tender. Add tomatoes, seasoning mix and liquid smoke. Cover and simmer for an additional 30 minutes. Uncover beans and continue to simmer about 1 hour longer or until soup thickens.

Holiday Bean Soup
Makes about 5 servings

1 jar Holiday Bean Soup Mix   2 cans (14 1/2 oz. each)
1 tsp. liquid smoke (optional)   stewed tomatoes

Remove seasoning bag from Holiday Bean Soup Mix and set aside. Rinse beans and place in a large soup pot. Pour 4 cups boiling water over beans, cover and let soak overnight. Drain water. Add 6 cups water. Cover and bring to a boil over high heat, stirring occasionally. Reduce heat to low and simmer 1 to 1 1/2 hours or until beans are tender. Add tomatoes, seasoning mix and liquid smoke. Cover and simmer for an additional 30 minutes. Uncover beans and continue to simmer about 1 hour longer or until soup thickens.

Holiday Bean Soup
Makes about 5 servings

1 jar Holiday Bean Soup Mix   2 cans (14 1/2 oz. each)
1 tsp. liquid smoke (optional)   stewed tomatoes

Remove seasoning bag from Holiday Bean Soup Mix and set aside. Rinse beans and place in a large soup pot. Pour 4 cups boiling water over beans, cover and let soak overnight. Drain water. Add 6 cups water. Cover and bring to a boil over high heat, stirring occasionally. Reduce heat to low and simmer 1 to 1 1/2 hours or until beans are tender. Add tomatoes, seasoning mix and liquid smoke. Cover and simmer for an additional 30 minutes. Uncover beans and continue to simmer about 1 hour longer or until soup thickens.

Holiday Bean Soup
Makes about 5 servings

1 jar Holiday Bean Soup Mix   2 cans (14 1/2 oz. each)
1 tsp. liquid smoke (optional)   stewed tomatoes

Remove seasoning bag from Holiday Bean Soup Mix and set aside. Rinse beans and place in a large soup pot. Pour 4 cups boiling water over beans, cover and let soak overnight. Drain water. Add 6 cups water. Cover and bring to a boil over high heat, stirring occasionally. Reduce heat to low and simmer 1 to 1 1/2 hours or until beans are tender. Add tomatoes, seasoning mix and liquid smoke. Cover and simmer for an additional 30 minutes. Uncover beans and continue to simmer about 1 hour longer or until soup thickens.

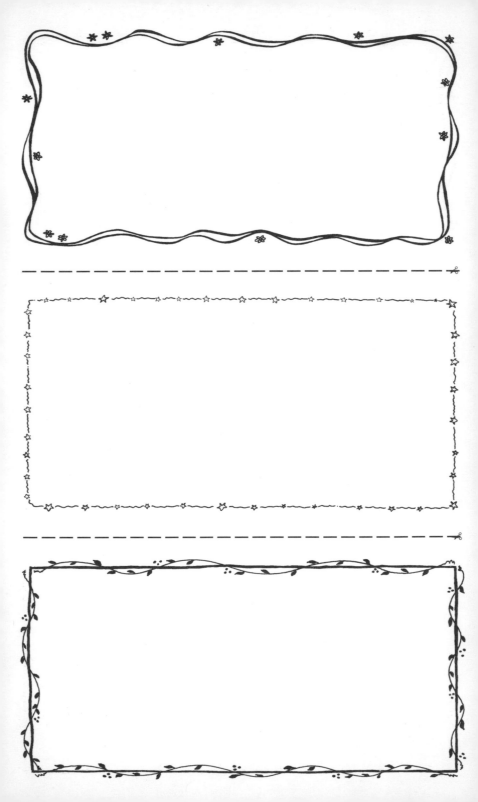

Holiday Bean Soup
Makes about 5 servings

1 jar Holiday Bean Soup Mix   2 cans (14 1/2 oz. each)
1 tsp. liquid smoke (optional)   stewed tomatoes

Remove seasoning bag from Holiday Bean Soup Mix and set aside. Rinse beans and place in a large soup pot. Pour 4 cups boiling water over beans, cover and let soak overnight. Drain water. Add 6 cups water. Cover and bring to a boil over high heat, stirring occasionally. Reduce heat to low and simmer 1 to 1 1/2 hours or until beans are tender. Add tomatoes, seasoning mix and liquid smoke. Cover and simmer for an additional 30 minutes. Uncover beans and continue to simmer about 1 hour longer or until soup thickens.

- ✂

Holiday Bean Soup
Makes about 5 servings

1 jar Holiday Bean Soup Mix   2 cans (14 1/2 oz. each)
1 tsp. liquid smoke (optional)   stewed tomatoes

Remove seasoning bag from Holiday Bean Soup Mix and set aside. Rinse beans and place in a large soup pot. Pour 4 cups boiling water over beans, cover and let soak overnight. Drain water. Add 6 cups water. Cover and bring to a boil over high heat, stirring occasionally. Reduce heat to low and simmer 1 to 1 1/2 hours or until beans are tender. Add tomatoes, seasoning mix and liquid smoke. Cover and simmer for an additional 30 minutes. Uncover beans and continue to simmer about 1 hour longer or until soup thickens.

- ✂

Holiday Bean Soup
Makes about 5 servings

1 jar Holiday Bean Soup Mix   2 cans (14 1/2 oz. each)
1 tsp. liquid smoke (optional)   stewed tomatoes

Remove seasoning bag from Holiday Bean Soup Mix and set aside. Rinse beans and place in a large soup pot. Pour 4 cups boiling water over beans, cover and let soak overnight. Drain water. Add 6 cups water. Cover and bring to a boil over high heat, stirring occasionally. Reduce heat to low and simmer 1 to 1 1/2 hours or until beans are tender. Add tomatoes, seasoning mix and liquid smoke. Cover and simmer for an additional 30 minutes. Uncover beans and continue to simmer about 1 hour longer or until soup thickens.

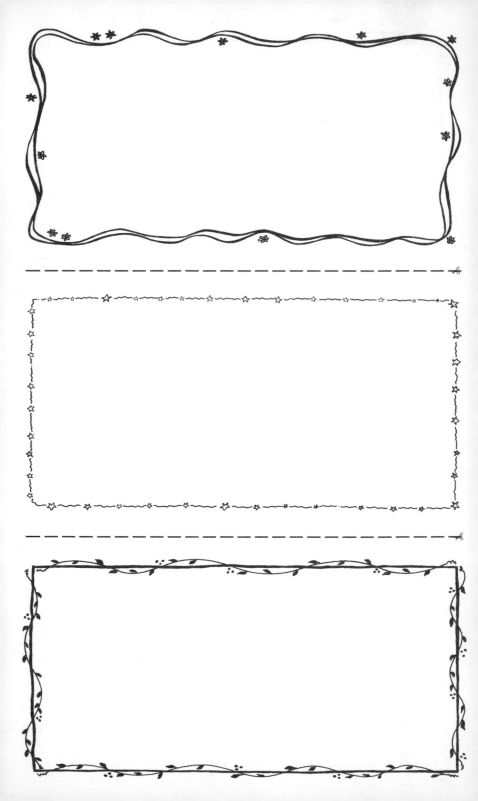

Holiday Hazelnut Cookie Mix

1 C. chopped hazelnuts, toasted and cooled completely*
1/2 C. dark brown sugar
1 C. biscuit and baking mix
1/2 C. light brown sugar
1 C. biscuit and baking mix

Layer the ingredients in the order given into a wide-mouth 1-quart canning jar. Pack each layer into place before adding the next ingredient.

Attach a gift tag with the mixing and baking directions.

*To toast hazelnuts, place nuts in a single layer on a baking sheet. Bake at 350°F for approximately 10 minutes or until nuts are golden brown.

Holiday Hazelnut Cookies

1 jar Holiday Hazelnut Cookie
   Mix
1/2 C. butter or margarine,
   melted
1 egg
1 tsp. vanilla

Preheat the oven to 375°F. In a medium bowl, cream the butter, egg and vanilla. Add the Holiday Hazelnut Cookie Mix and stir until well blended. Shape into 1-inch balls. Place on a greased baking sheet. Bake for 10 to 12 minutes or until cookies are a light golden brown. Transfer to wire racks to cool.

Holiday Hazelnut Cookies

1 jar Holiday Hazelnut Cookie
  Mix
1/2 C. butter or margarine,
  melted

1 egg
1 tsp. vanilla

    Preheat the oven to 375°F. In a medium bowl, cream the butter, egg and vanilla. Add the Holiday Hazelnut Cookie Mix and stir until well blended. Shape into 1-inch balls. Place on a greased baking sheet. Bake for 10 to 12 minutes or until cookies are a light golden brown. Transfer to wire racks to cool.

Holiday Hazelnut Cookies

1 jar Holiday Hazelnut Cookie
  Mix
1/2 C. butter or margarine,
  melted

1 egg
1 tsp. vanilla

    Preheat the oven to 375°F. In a medium bowl, cream the butter, egg and vanilla. Add the Holiday Hazelnut Cookie Mix and stir until well blended. Shape into 1-inch balls. Place on a greased baking sheet. Bake for 10 to 12 minutes or until cookies are a light golden brown. Transfer to wire racks to cool.

Holiday Hazelnut Cookies

1 jar Holiday Hazelnut Cookie
  Mix
1/2 C. butter or margarine,
  melted

1 egg
1 tsp. vanilla

    Preheat the oven to 375°F. In a medium bowl, cream the butter, egg and vanilla. Add the Holiday Hazelnut Cookie Mix and stir until well blended. Shape into 1-inch balls. Place on a greased baking sheet. Bake for 10 to 12 minutes or until cookies are a light golden brown. Transfer to wire racks to cool.

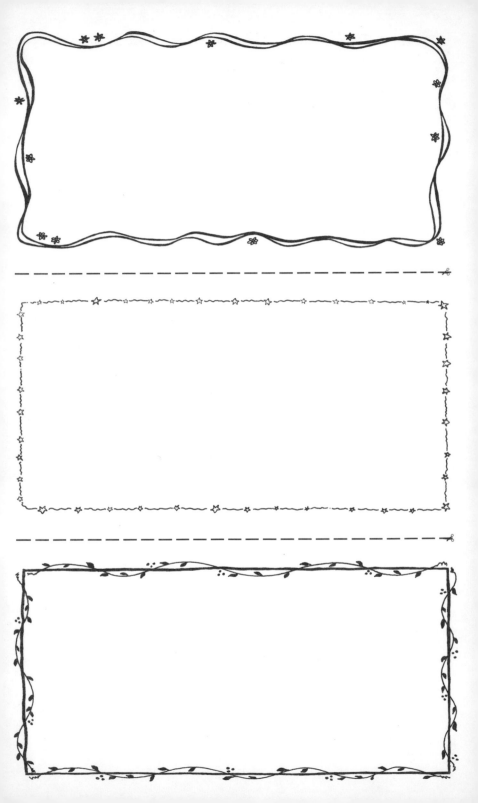

Holiday Hazelnut Cookies

1 jar Holiday Hazelnut Cookie
  Mix
1/2 C. butter or margarine,
  melted

1 egg
1 tsp. vanilla

    Preheat the oven to 375°F. In a medium bowl, cream the butter, egg and vanilla. Add the Holiday Hazelnut Cookie Mix and stir until well blended. Shape into 1-inch balls. Place on a greased baking sheet. Bake for 10 to 12 minutes or until cookies are a light golden brown. Transfer to wire racks to cool.

Holiday Hazelnut Cookies

1 jar Holiday Hazelnut Cookie
  Mix
1/2 C. butter or margarine,
  melted

1 egg
1 tsp. vanilla

    Preheat the oven to 375°F. In a medium bowl, cream the butter, egg and vanilla. Add the Holiday Hazelnut Cookie Mix and stir until well blended. Shape into 1-inch balls. Place on a greased baking sheet. Bake for 10 to 12 minutes or until cookies are a light golden brown. Transfer to wire racks to cool.

Holiday Hazelnut Cookies

1 jar Holiday Hazelnut Cookie
  Mix
1/2 C. butter or margarine,
  melted

1 egg
1 tsp. vanilla

    Preheat the oven to 375°F. In a medium bowl, cream the butter, egg and vanilla. Add the Holiday Hazelnut Cookie Mix and stir until well blended. Shape into 1-inch balls. Place on a greased baking sheet. Bake for 10 to 12 minutes or until cookies are a light golden brown. Transfer to wire racks to cool.

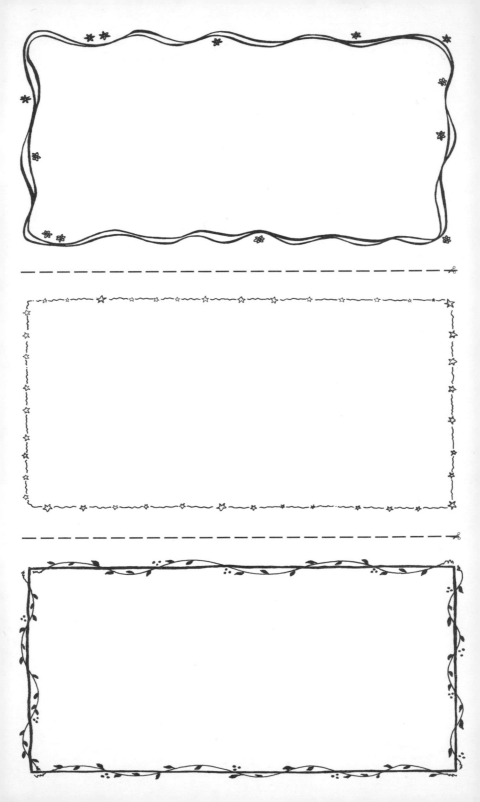

Pumpkin Mini Muffin Mix

2 1/4 C. all-purpose flour
3 tsp. baking powder
1 1/8 tsp. salt
3/4 C. sugar
3/4 tsp. cinnamon
3/4 tsp. nutmeg
3/4 C. raisins

Layer the ingredients in the order given into a wide-mouth 1-quart canning jar. Pack each layer into place before adding the next ingredient.

Attach a gift tag with the mixing and baking directions.

Pumpkin Mini Muffins

Makes 2 to 3 dozen

1 jar Pumpkin Mini Muffin Mix
1/4 C. shortening
1 egg, beaten
1/2 C. canned pumpkin
1/2 C. milk

Preheat the oven to 400°F. In a large bowl, place the Pumpkin Mini Muffin Mix. Cut in the shortening until crumbly. Add the egg, pumpkin and milk. Stir until the mixture is well blended. Fill greased or paper lined mini muffin pans 2/3 full. Bake for 15 to 20 minutes or until done.

Pumpkin Mini Muffins
Makes 2 to 3 dozen

1 jar Pumpkin Mini Muffin Mix   1/2 C. canned pumpkin
1/4 C. shortening   1/2 C. milk
1 egg, beaten

Preheat the oven to 400°F. In a large bowl, place the Pumpkin Mini Muffin Mix. Cut in the shortening until crumbly. Add the egg, pumpkin and milk. Stir until the mixture is well blended. Fill greased or paper lined mini muffin pans 2/3 full. Bake for 15 to 20 minutes or until done.

Pumpkin Mini Muffins
Makes 2 to 3 dozen

1 jar Pumpkin Mini Muffin Mix   1/2 C. canned pumpkin
1/4 C. shortening   1/2 C. milk
1 egg, beaten

Preheat the oven to 400°F. In a large bowl, place the Pumpkin Mini Muffin Mix. Cut in the shortening until crumbly. Add the egg, pumpkin and milk. Stir until the mixture is well blended. Fill greased or paper lined mini muffin pans 2/3 full. Bake for 15 to 20 minutes or until done.

Pumpkin Mini Muffins
Makes 2 to 3 dozen

1 jar Pumpkin Mini Muffin Mix   1/2 C. canned pumpkin
1/4 C. shortening   1/2 C. milk
1 egg, beaten

Preheat the oven to 400°F. In a large bowl, place the Pumpkin Mini Muffin Mix. Cut in the shortening until crumbly. Add the egg, pumpkin and milk. Stir until the mixture is well blended. Fill greased or paper lined mini muffin pans 2/3 full. Bake for 15 to 20 minutes or until done.

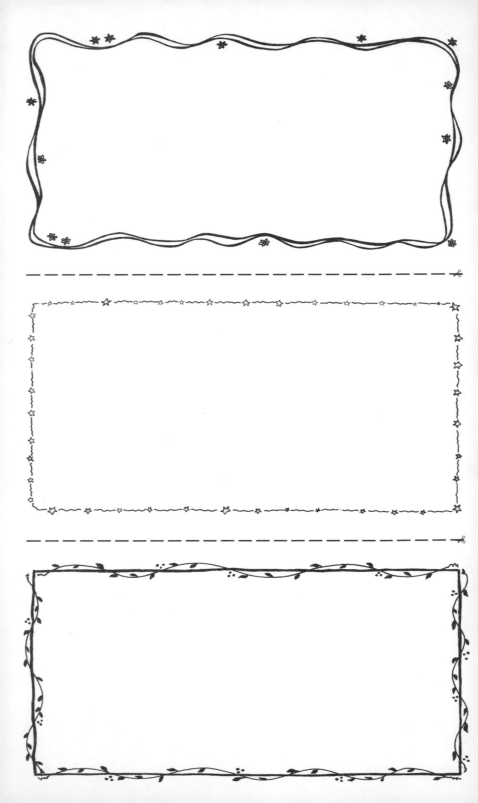

Pumpkin Mini Muffins
Makes 2 to 3 dozen

1 jar Pumpkin Mini Muffin Mix   1/2 C. canned pumpkin
1/4 C. shortening   1/2 C. milk
1 egg, beaten

Preheat the oven to 400°F. In a large bowl, place the Pumpkin Mini Muffin Mix. Cut in the shortening until crumbly. Add the egg, pumpkin and milk. Stir until the mixture is well blended. Fill greased or paper lined mini muffin pans 2/3 full. Bake for 15 to 20 minutes or until done.

Pumpkin Mini Muffins
Makes 2 to 3 dozen

1 jar Pumpkin Mini Muffin Mix   1/2 C. canned pumpkin
1/4 C. shortening   1/2 C. milk
1 egg, beaten

Preheat the oven to 400°F. In a large bowl, place the Pumpkin Mini Muffin Mix. Cut in the shortening until crumbly. Add the egg, pumpkin and milk. Stir until the mixture is well blended. Fill greased or paper lined mini muffin pans 2/3 full. Bake for 15 to 20 minutes or until done.

Pumpkin Mini Muffins
Makes 2 to 3 dozen

1 jar Pumpkin Mini Muffin Mix   1/2 C. canned pumpkin
1/4 C. shortening   1/2 C. milk
1 egg, beaten

Preheat the oven to 400°F. In a large bowl, place the Pumpkin Mini Muffin Mix. Cut in the shortening until crumbly. Add the egg, pumpkin and milk. Stir until the mixture is well blended. Fill greased or paper lined mini muffin pans 2/3 full. Bake for 15 to 20 minutes or until done.

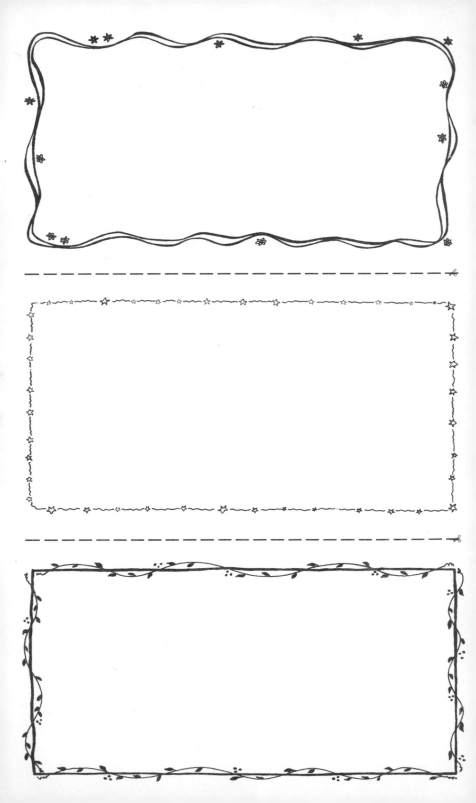

Cranberry Pecan Crunch Cookie Mix

2/3 C. sweetened dried
   cranberries
1/2 C. chopped pecans,
   toasted and cooled
   completely*
1/2 C. dark brown sugar
1 C. biscuit and baking mix
1/2 C. light brown sugar
1 C. biscuit and baking mix

Layer the ingredients in the order given into a wide-mouth 1-quart canning jar. Pack each layer into place before adding the next ingredient.

Attach a gift tag with the mixing and baking directions.

*To toast pecans, place nuts in a single layer on a baking sheet. Bake at 350°F for approximately 10 minutes or until nuts are golden brown.

Cranberry Pecan Crunch Cookies

1 jar Cranberry Pecan Crunch
   Cookie Mix
1/2 C. butter or margarine,
   melted
1 egg
1 tsp. vanilla

Preheat the oven to 375°F. In a medium bowl, cream the butter, egg and vanilla. Add the Cranberry Pecan Crunch Cookie Mix and stir until well blended. Shape into 1-inch balls. Place on a greased baking sheet. Bake for 10 to 12 minutes or until cookies are a light golden brown. Transfer to wire racks to cool.

Cranberry Pecan Crunch Cookies

1 jar Cranberry Pecan Crunch
    Cookie Mix
1/2 C. butter or margarine,
    melted

1 egg
1 tsp. vanilla

    Preheat the oven to 375°F. In a medium bowl, cream the butter, egg and vanilla. Add the Cranberry Pecan Crunch Cookie Mix and stir until well blended. Shape into 1-inch balls. Place on a greased baking sheet. Bake for 10 to 12 minutes or until cookies are a light golden brown. Transfer to wire racks to cool.

Cranberry Pecan Crunch Cookies

1 jar Cranberry Pecan Crunch
    Cookie Mix
1/2 C. butter or margarine,
    melted

1 egg
1 tsp. vanilla

    Preheat the oven to 375°F. In a medium bowl, cream the butter, egg and vanilla. Add the Cranberry Pecan Crunch Cookie Mix and stir until well blended. Shape into 1-inch balls. Place on a greased baking sheet. Bake for 10 to 12 minutes or until cookies are a light golden brown. Transfer to wire racks to cool.

Cranberry Pecan Crunch Cookies

1 jar Cranberry Pecan Crunch
    Cookie Mix
1/2 C. butter or margarine,
    melted

1 egg
1 tsp. vanilla

    Preheat the oven to 375°F. In a medium bowl, cream the butter, egg and vanilla. Add the Cranberry Pecan Crunch Cookie Mix and stir until well blended. Shape into 1-inch balls. Place on a greased baking sheet. Bake for 10 to 12 minutes or until cookies are a light golden brown. Transfer to wire racks to cool.

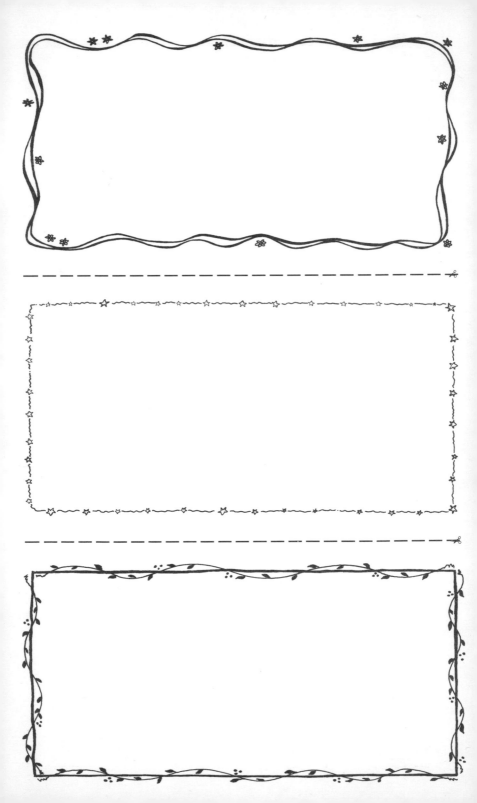

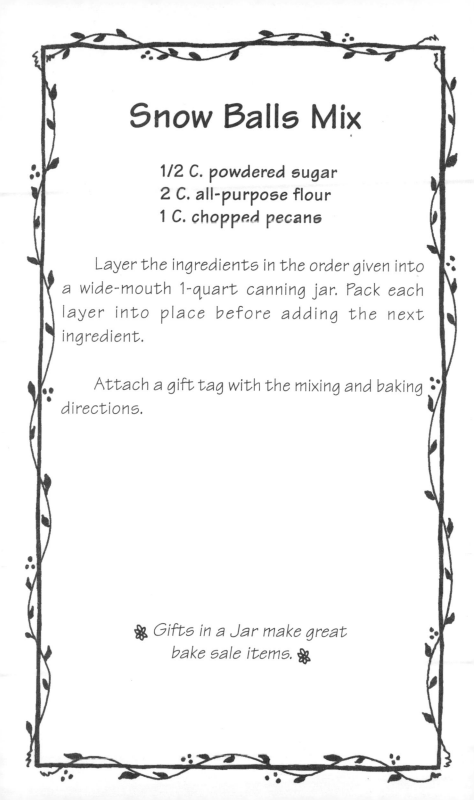

Snow Balls Mix

1/2 C. powdered sugar
2 C. all-purpose flour
1 C. chopped pecans

Layer the ingredients in the order given into a wide-mouth 1-quart canning jar. Pack each layer into place before adding the next ingredient.

Attach a gift tag with the mixing and baking directions.

❀ Gifts in a Jar make great bake sale items. ❀

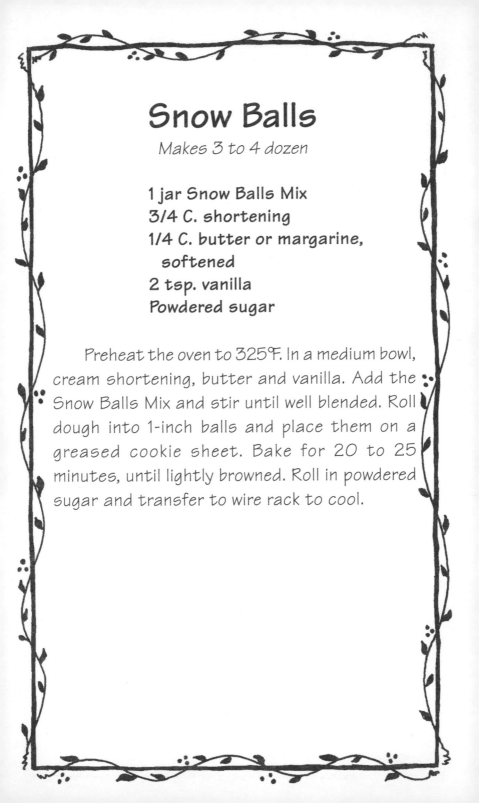

Snow Balls

Makes 3 to 4 dozen

1 jar Snow Balls Mix
3/4 C. shortening
1/4 C. butter or margarine,
  softened
2 tsp. vanilla
Powdered sugar

Preheat the oven to 325°F. In a medium bowl, cream shortening, butter and vanilla. Add the Snow Balls Mix and stir until well blended. Roll dough into 1-inch balls and place them on a greased cookie sheet. Bake for 20 to 25 minutes, until lightly browned. Roll in powdered sugar and transfer to wire rack to cool.

Snow Balls
Makes 3 to 4 dozen

1 jar Snow Balls Mix
3/4 C. shortening
1/4 C. butter or margarine,
  softened

2 tsp. vanilla
Powdered sugar

   Preheat the oven to 325°F. In a medium bowl, cream shortening, butter and vanilla. Add the Snow Balls Mix and stir until well blended. Roll dough into 1-inch balls and place them on a greased cookie sheet. Bake for 20 to 25 minutes, until lightly browned. Roll in powdered sugar and transfer to wire rack to cool.

Snow Balls
Makes 3 to 4 dozen

1 jar Snow Balls Mix
3/4 C. shortening
1/4 C. butter or margarine,
  softened

2 tsp. vanilla
Powdered sugar

   Preheat the oven to 325°F. In a medium bowl, cream shortening, butter and vanilla. Add the Snow Balls Mix and stir until well blended. Roll dough into 1-inch balls and place them on a greased cookie sheet. Bake for 20 to 25 minutes, until lightly browned. Roll in powdered sugar and transfer to wire rack to cool.

Snow Balls
Makes 3 to 4 dozen

1 jar Snow Balls Mix
3/4 C. shortening
1/4 C. butter or margarine,
  softened

2 tsp. vanilla
Powdered sugar

   Preheat the oven to 325°F. In a medium bowl, cream shortening, butter and vanilla. Add the Snow Balls Mix and stir until well blended. Roll dough into 1-inch balls and place them on a greased cookie sheet. Bake for 20 to 25 minutes, until lightly browned. Roll in powdered sugar and transfer to wire rack to cool.

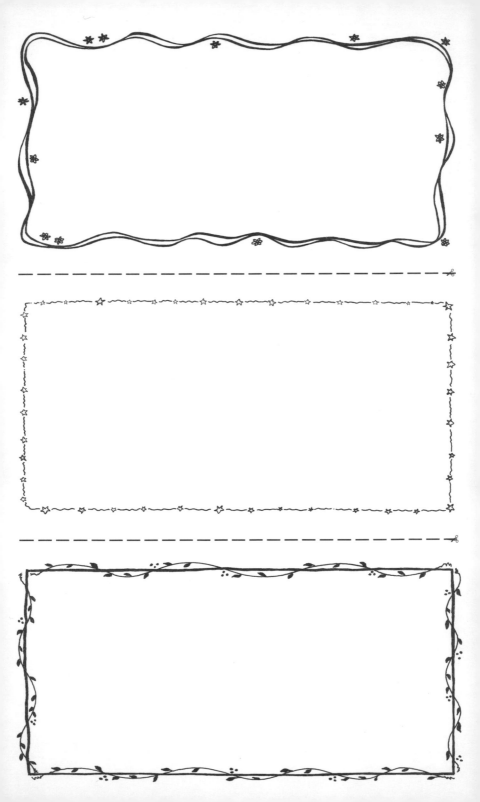

Snow Balls
Makes 3 to 4 dozen

1 jar Snow Balls Mix
3/4 C. shortening
1/4 C. butter or margarine,
    softened

2 tsp. vanilla
Powdered sugar

Preheat the oven to 325°F. In a medium bowl, cream shortening, butter and vanilla. Add the Snow Balls Mix and stir until well blended. Roll dough into 1-inch balls and place them on a greased cookie sheet. Bake for 20 to 25 minutes, until lightly browned. Roll in powdered sugar and transfer to wire rack to cool.

Snow Balls
Makes 3 to 4 dozen

1 jar Snow Balls Mix
3/4 C. shortening
1/4 C. butter or margarine,
    softened

2 tsp. vanilla
Powdered sugar

Preheat the oven to 325°F. In a medium bowl, cream shortening, butter and vanilla. Add the Snow Balls Mix and stir until well blended. Roll dough into 1-inch balls and place them on a greased cookie sheet. Bake for 20 to 25 minutes, until lightly browned. Roll in powdered sugar and transfer to wire rack to cool.

Snow Balls
Makes 3 to 4 dozen

1 jar Snow Balls Mix
3/4 C. shortening
1/4 C. butter or margarine,
    softened

2 tsp. vanilla
Powdered sugar

Preheat the oven to 325°F. In a medium bowl, cream shortening, butter and vanilla. Add the Snow Balls Mix and stir until well blended. Roll dough into 1-inch balls and place them on a greased cookie sheet. Bake for 20 to 25 minutes, until lightly browned. Roll in powdered sugar and transfer to wire rack to cool.

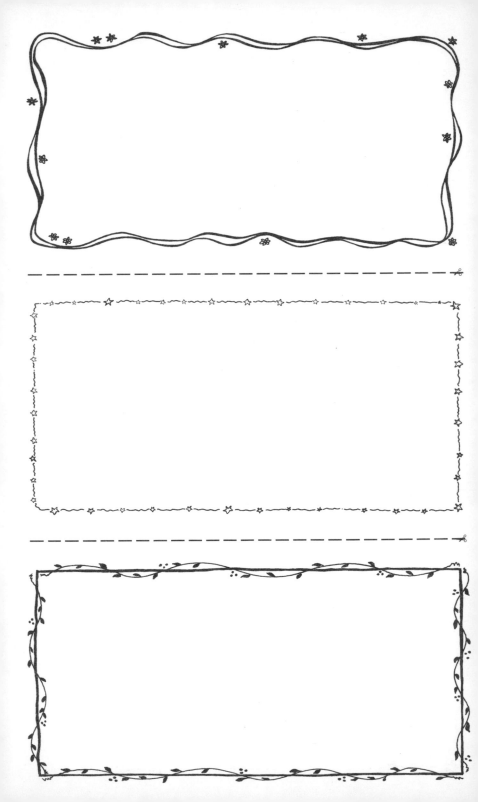

Gingerbread Cookie Mix

2 C. all-purpose flour
1 tsp. baking powder
1 tsp. baking soda
1 C. brown sugar
1 1/2 C. all-purpose flour
2 tsp. ginger
1 tsp. ground cloves
1 tsp. cinnamon
1 tsp. allspice

Layer the ingredients in the order given into a wide-mouth 1-quart canning jar. Pack each layer into place before adding the next ingredient.

Attach a gift tag with the mixing and baking directions.

❊ For the Gingerbread Cookie Mix, tie a gingerbread man cookie cutter or a gingerbread man ornament to the mix. ❊

Gingerbread Cookies

Makes 1 1/2 to 2 dozen

1 jar Gingerbread Cookie Mix
1/2 C. butter or margarine,
   softened
3/4 C. molasses
1 egg, slightly beaten

In a large bowl, place Gingerbread Cookie Mix. Stir to blend ingredients together. Mix in butter, molasses and egg until well blended. Dough will be very stiff, so you may need to use your hands. Cover and refrigerate for 1 hour. Preheat the oven to 350°F. Roll dough to 1/4 inch thick on a lightly floured surface. Cut into shapes with a cookie cutter. Place cookies on a lightly greased cookie sheet about 2 inches apart. Bake for 10 to 12 minutes. Transfer to wire racks to cool. Decorate as desired.

Gingerbread Cookies
Makes 1 1/2 to 2 dozen

1 jar Gingerbread Cookie Mix
1/2 C. butter or margarine,
softened

3/4 C. molasses
1 egg, slightly beaten

In a large bowl, place Gingerbread Cookie Mix. Stir to blend ingredients together. Mix in butter, molasses and egg until well blended. Dough will be very stiff, so you may need to use your hands. Cover and refrigerate for 1 hour. Preheat the oven to 350°F. Roll dough to 1/4 inch thick on a lightly floured surface. Cut into shapes with a cookie cutter. Place cookies on a lightly greased cookie sheet about 2 inches apart. Bake for 10 to 12 minutes. Transfer to wire racks to cool. Decorate as desired.

Gingerbread Cookies
Makes 1 1/2 to 2 dozen

1 jar Gingerbread Cookie Mix
1/2 C. butter or margarine,
softened

3/4 C. molasses
1 egg, slightly beaten

In a large bowl, place Gingerbread Cookie Mix. Stir to blend ingredients together. Mix in butter, molasses and egg until well blended. Dough will be very stiff, so you may need to use your hands. Cover and refrigerate for 1 hour. Preheat the oven to 350°F. Roll dough to 1/4 inch thick on a lightly floured surface. Cut into shapes with a cookie cutter. Place cookies on a lightly greased cookie sheet about 2 inches apart. Bake for 10 to 12 minutes. Transfer to wire racks to cool. Decorate as desired.

Gingerbread Cookies
Makes 1 1/2 to 2 dozen

1 jar Gingerbread Cookie Mix
1/2 C. butter or margarine,
softened

3/4 C. molasses
1 egg, slightly beaten

In a large bowl, place Gingerbread Cookie Mix. Stir to blend ingredients together. Mix in butter, molasses and egg until well blended. Dough will be very stiff, so you may need to use your hands. Cover and refrigerate for 1 hour. Preheat the oven to 350°F. Roll dough to 1/4 inch thick on a lightly floured surface. Cut into shapes with a cookie cutter. Place cookies on a lightly greased cookie sheet about 2 inches apart. Bake for 10 to 12 minutes. Transfer to wire racks to cool. Decorate as desired.

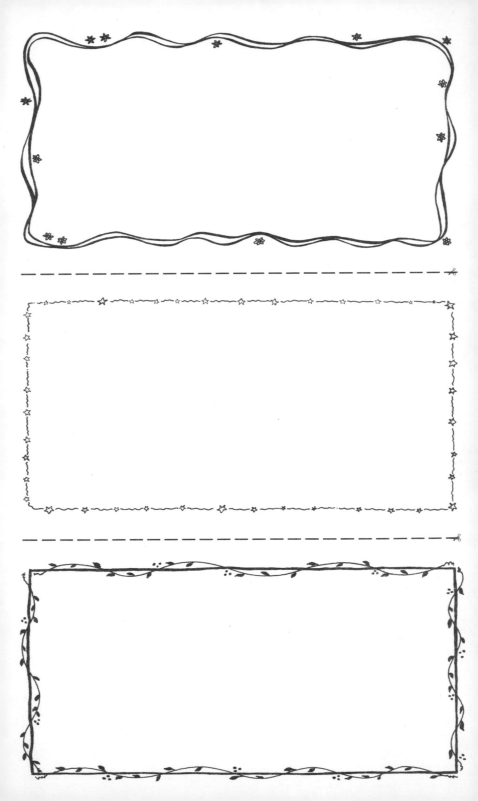

Gingerbread Cookies
Makes 1 1/2 to 2 dozen

1 jar Gingerbread Cookie Mix
1/2 C. butter or margarine,
   softened

3/4 C. molasses
1 egg, slightly beaten

In a large bowl, place Gingerbread Cookie Mix. Stir to blend ingredients together. Mix in butter, molasses and egg until well blended. Dough will be very stiff, so you may need to use your hands. Cover and refrigerate for 1 hour. Preheat the oven to 350°F. Roll dough to 1/4 inch thick on a lightly floured surface. Cut into shapes with a cookie cutter. Place cookies on a lightly greased cookie sheet about 2 inches apart. Bake for 10 to 12 minutes. Transfer to wire racks to cool. Decorate as desired.

Gingerbread Cookies
Makes 1 1/2 to 2 dozen

1 jar Gingerbread Cookie Mix
1/2 C. butter or margarine,
   softened

3/4 C. molasses
1 egg, slightly beaten

In a large bowl, place Gingerbread Cookie Mix. Stir to blend ingredients together. Mix in butter, molasses and egg until well blended. Dough will be very stiff, so you may need to use your hands. Cover and refrigerate for 1 hour. Preheat the oven to 350°F. Roll dough to 1/4 inch thick on a lightly floured surface. Cut into shapes with a cookie cutter. Place cookies on a lightly greased cookie sheet about 2 inches apart. Bake for 10 to 12 minutes. Transfer to wire racks to cool. Decorate as desired.

Gingerbread Cookies
Makes 1 1/2 to 2 dozen

1 jar Gingerbread Cookie Mix
1/2 C. butter or margarine,
   softened

3/4 C. molasses
1 egg, slightly beaten

In a large bowl, place Gingerbread Cookie Mix. Stir to blend ingredients together. Mix in butter, molasses and egg until well blended. Dough will be very stiff, so you may need to use your hands. Cover and refrigerate for 1 hour. Preheat the oven to 350°F. Roll dough to 1/4 inch thick on a lightly floured surface. Cut into shapes with a cookie cutter. Place cookies on a lightly greased cookie sheet about 2 inches apart. Bake for 10 to 12 minutes. Transfer to wire racks to cool. Decorate as desired.

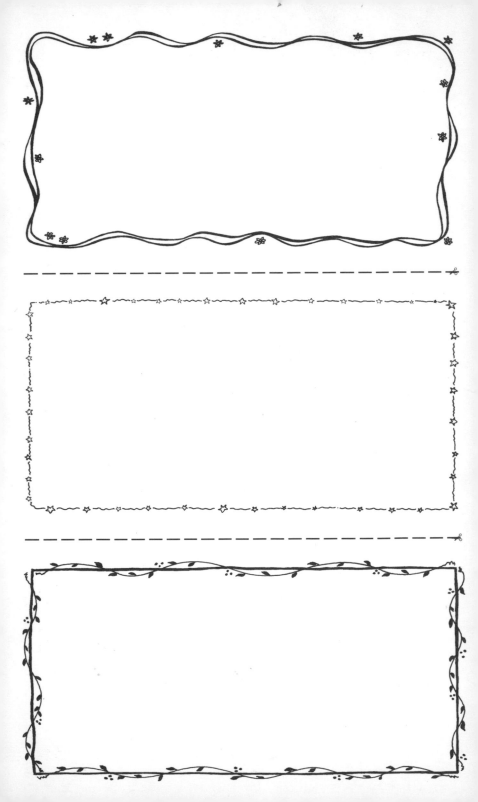

Cranberry Hootycreeks Mix

1/2 C. plus 2 T. all-purpose flour
1/2 C. old-fashioned oats
1/2 C. all-purpose flour
1/2 tsp. baking soda
1/2 tsp. salt
1/3 C. brown sugar
1/3 C. sugar
1/2 C. dried cranberries
1/2 C. white chocolate chips
1/2 C. chopped pecans

Layer the ingredients in the order given into a wide-mouth 1-quart canning jar. Pack each layer into place before adding the next ingredient.

Attach a gift tag with the mixing and baking directions.

❀ At times, it may seem impossible to make all of the jar ingredients fit, but with persistence, they do all fit. ❀

Cranberry Hootycreeks

Makes 1 1/2 to 2 dozen

1 jar Cranberry Hootycreeks
   Mix
1/2 C. butter or margarine,
   softened
1 egg
1 tsp. vanilla

Preheat the oven to 350°F. In a large bowl, cream butter, egg and vanilla. Add the Cranberry Hootycreeks Mix and mix together by hand until the mixture is well blended. Drop by heaping tablespoonfuls onto a greased cookie sheet. Bake for 8 to 10 minutes or until the edges start to brown. Transfer to wire racks to cool.

Cranberry Hootycreeks
Makes 1 1/2 to 2 dozen

1 jar Cranberry Hootycreeks Mix
1/2 C. butter or margarine,
    softened

1 egg
1 tsp. vanilla

Preheat the oven to 350°F. In a large bowl, cream butter, egg and vanilla. Add the Cranberry Hootycreeks Mix and mix together by hand until the mixture is well blended. Drop by heaping tablespoonfuls onto a greased cookie sheet. Bake for 8 to 10 minutes or until the edges start to brown. Transfer to wire racks to cool.

Cranberry Hootycreeks
Makes 1 1/2 to 2 dozen

1 jar Cranberry Hootycreeks Mix
1/2 C. butter or margarine,
    softened

1 egg
1 tsp. vanilla

Preheat the oven to 350°F. In a large bowl, cream butter, egg and vanilla. Add the Cranberry Hootycreeks Mix and mix together by hand until the mixture is well blended. Drop by heaping tablespoonfuls onto a greased cookie sheet. Bake for 8 to 10 minutes or until the edges start to brown. Transfer to wire racks to cool.

Cranberry Hootycreeks
Makes 1 1/2 to 2 dozen

1 jar Cranberry Hootycreeks Mix
1/2 C. butter or margarine,
    softened

1 egg
1 tsp. vanilla

Preheat the oven to 350°F. In a large bowl, cream butter, egg and vanilla. Add the Cranberry Hootycreeks Mix and mix together by hand until the mixture is well blended. Drop by heaping tablespoonfuls onto a greased cookie sheet. Bake for 8 to 10 minutes or until the edges start to brown. Transfer to wire racks to cool.

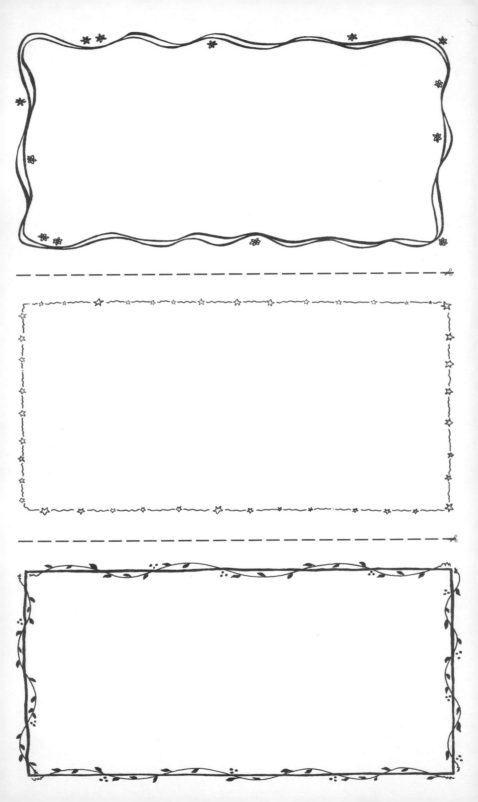

Cookie Jar Sugar Cookies
Makes 1 to 2 dozen

1 jar Cookie Jar Sugar Cookie Mix
1 egg
3/4 C. butter or margarine, softened

6 T. sour cream
3/4 tsp. vanilla

In a large bowl, cream egg and butter until light and fluffy. Add sour cream, vanilla and the Cookie Jar Sugar Cookie Mix. Using an electric mixer at a low speed, mix until combined. Use hands if necessary. Cover dough and refrigerate for several hours or overnight. Remove dough from the refrigerator. Preheat the oven to 375°F. On a lightly floured surface, roll chilled dough to 1/8 inch thick. Cut dough into desired shapes. Place on an ungreased cookie sheet and bake for 10 to 12 minutes. Transfer to wire racks to cool.

Cookie Jar Sugar Cookies
Makes 1 to 2 dozen

1 jar Cookie Jar Sugar Cookie Mix
1 egg
3/4 C. butter or margarine, softened

6 T. sour cream
3/4 tsp. vanilla

In a large bowl, cream egg and butter until light and fluffy. Add sour cream, vanilla and the Cookie Jar Sugar Cookie Mix. Using an electric mixer at a low speed, mix until combined. Use hands if necessary. Cover dough and refrigerate for several hours or overnight. Remove dough from the refrigerator. Preheat the oven to 375°F. On a lightly floured surface, roll chilled dough to 1/8 inch thick. Cut dough into desired shapes. Place on an ungreased cookie sheet and bake for 10 to 12 minutes. Transfer to wire racks to cool.

Cookie Jar Sugar Cookies
Makes 1 to 2 dozen

1 jar Cookie Jar Sugar Cookie Mix
1 egg
3/4 C. butter or margarine, softened

6 T. sour cream
3/4 tsp. vanilla

In a large bowl, cream egg and butter until light and fluffy. Add sour cream, vanilla and the Cookie Jar Sugar Cookie Mix. Using an electric mixer at a low speed, mix until combined. Use hands if necessary. Cover dough and refrigerate for several hours or overnight. Remove dough from the refrigerator. Preheat the oven to 375°F. On a lightly floured surface, roll chilled dough to 1/8 inch thick. Cut dough into desired shapes. Place on an ungreased cookie sheet and bake for 10 to 12 minutes. Transfer to wire racks to cool.

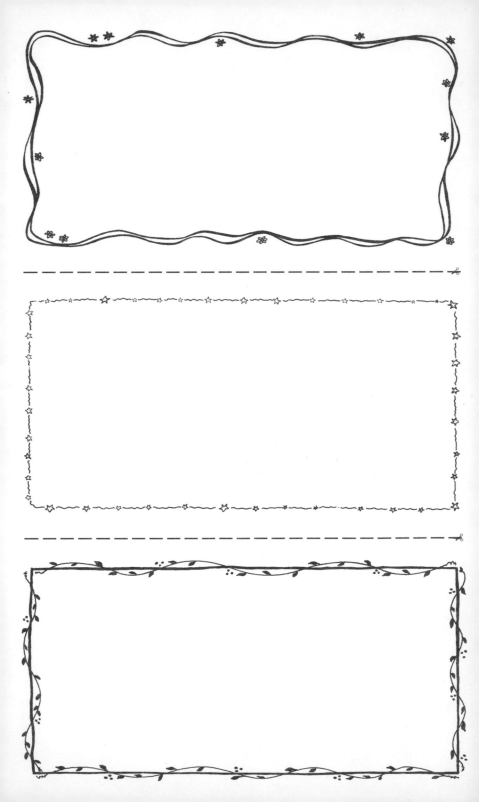

Cookie Jar Sugar Cookies
Makes 1 to 2 dozen

1 jar Cookie Jar Sugar Cookie Mix   6 T. sour cream
1 egg   3/4 tsp. vanilla
3/4 C. butter or margarine, softened

In a large bowl, cream egg and butter until light and fluffy. Add sour cream, vanilla and the Cookie Jar Sugar Cookie Mix. Using an electric mixer at a low speed, mix until combined. Use hands if necessary. Cover dough and refrigerate for several hours or overnight. Remove dough from the refrigerator. Preheat the oven to 375°F. On a lightly floured surface, roll chilled dough to 1/8 inch thick. Cut dough into desired shapes. Place on an ungreased cookie sheet and bake for 10 to 12 minutes. Transfer to wire racks to cool.

Cookie Jar Sugar Cookies
Makes 1 to 2 dozen

1 jar Cookie Jar Sugar Cookie Mix   6 T. sour cream
1 egg   3/4 tsp. vanilla
3/4 C. butter or margarine, softened

In a large bowl, cream egg and butter until light and fluffy. Add sour cream, vanilla and the Cookie Jar Sugar Cookie Mix. Using an electric mixer at a low speed, mix until combined. Use hands if necessary. Cover dough and refrigerate for several hours or overnight. Remove dough from the refrigerator. Preheat the oven to 375°F. On a lightly floured surface, roll chilled dough to 1/8 inch thick. Cut dough into desired shapes. Place on an ungreased cookie sheet and bake for 10 to 12 minutes. Transfer to wire racks to cool.

Cookie Jar Sugar Cookies
Makes 1 to 2 dozen

1 jar Cookie Jar Sugar Cookie Mix   6 T. sour cream
1 egg   3/4 tsp. vanilla
3/4 C. butter or margarine, softened

In a large bowl, cream egg and butter until light and fluffy. Add sour cream, vanilla and the Cookie Jar Sugar Cookie Mix. Using an electric mixer at a low speed, mix until combined. Use hands if necessary. Cover dough and refrigerate for several hours or overnight. Remove dough from the refrigerator. Preheat the oven to 375°F. On a lightly floured surface, roll chilled dough to 1/8 inch thick. Cut dough into desired shapes. Place on an ungreased cookie sheet and bake for 10 to 12 minutes. Transfer to wire racks to cool.

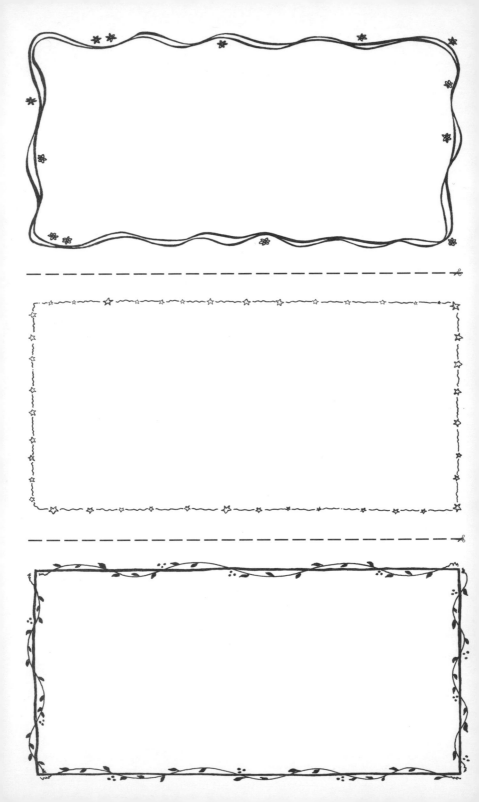

Blizzard Bites Mix

1 C. bite-size square rice cereal
3/4 C. broken mini twist pretzels
1/2 C. coarsely chopped
   macadamia nuts
1/2 C. coarsely chopped dried
   pineapple
1/2 C. sweetened dried
   cranberries
1/2 C. white baking chips (placed
   in a baggie)

Layer the ingredients in the order given into a wide-mouth 1-quart canning jar. Pack each layer into place before adding the next ingredient.

Attach a gift tag with the mixing directions.

❋ *For a special touch, attach a wooden spoon to the jar.* ❋

Blizzard Bites

1 jar Blizzard Bites Mix

Remove white baking chips from Blizzard Bites Mix and set aside. Place remaining contents into a medium bowl, stirring to combine. Place white baking chips in a small saucepan and melt over low heat. Pour melted white baking chips over snack mixture. Stir until snack mixture is evenly coated with melted white baking chips. Spread mixture in a single layer on waxed paper to harden. Store in an airtight container.

Blizzard Bites

1 jar Blizzard Bites Mix

Remove white baking chips from Blizzard Bites Mix and set aside. Place remaining contents into a medium bowl, stirring to combine. Place white baking chips in a small saucepan and melt over low heat. Pour melted white baking chips over snack mixture. Stir until snack mixture is evenly coated with melted white baking chips. Spread mixture in a single layer on waxed paper to harden. Store in an airtight container.

Blizzard Bites

1 jar Blizzard Bites Mix

Remove white baking chips from Blizzard Bites Mix and set aside. Place remaining contents into a medium bowl, stirring to combine. Place white baking chips in a small saucepan and melt over low heat. Pour melted white baking chips over snack mixture. Stir until snack mixture is evenly coated with melted white baking chips. Spread mixture in a single layer on waxed paper to harden. Store in an airtight container.

Blizzard Bites

1 jar Blizzard Bites Mix

Remove white baking chips from Blizzard Bites Mix and set aside. Place remaining contents into a medium bowl, stirring to combine. Place white baking chips in a small saucepan and melt over low heat. Pour melted white baking chips over snack mixture. Stir until snack mixture is evenly coated with melted white baking chips. Spread mixture in a single layer on waxed paper to harden. Store in an airtight container.

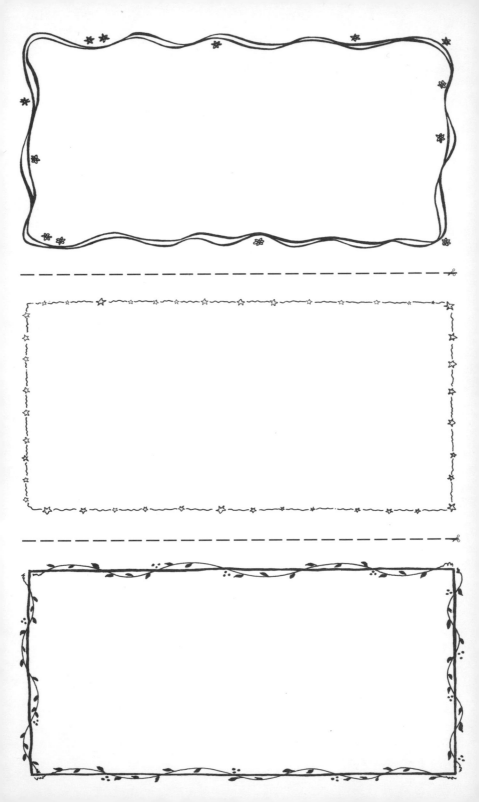

Blizzard Bites

1 jar Blizzard Bites Mix

Remove white baking chips from Blizzard Bites Mix and set aside. Place remaining contents into a medium bowl, stirring to combine. Place white baking chips in a small saucepan and melt over low heat. Pour melted white baking chips over snack mixture. Stir until snack mixture is evenly coated with melted white baking chips. Spread mixture in a single layer on waxed paper to harden. Store in an airtight container.

Blizzard Bites

1 jar Blizzard Bites Mix

Remove white baking chips from Blizzard Bites Mix and set aside. Place remaining contents into a medium bowl, stirring to combine. Place white baking chips in a small saucepan and melt over low heat. Pour melted white baking chips over snack mixture. Stir until snack mixture is evenly coated with melted white baking chips. Spread mixture in a single layer on waxed paper to harden. Store in an airtight container.

Blizzard Bites

1 jar Blizzard Bites Mix

Remove white baking chips from Blizzard Bites Mix and set aside. Place remaining contents into a medium bowl, stirring to combine. Place white baking chips in a small saucepan and melt over low heat. Pour melted white baking chips over snack mixture. Stir until snack mixture is evenly coated with melted white baking chips. Spread mixture in a single layer on waxed paper to harden. Store in an airtight container.

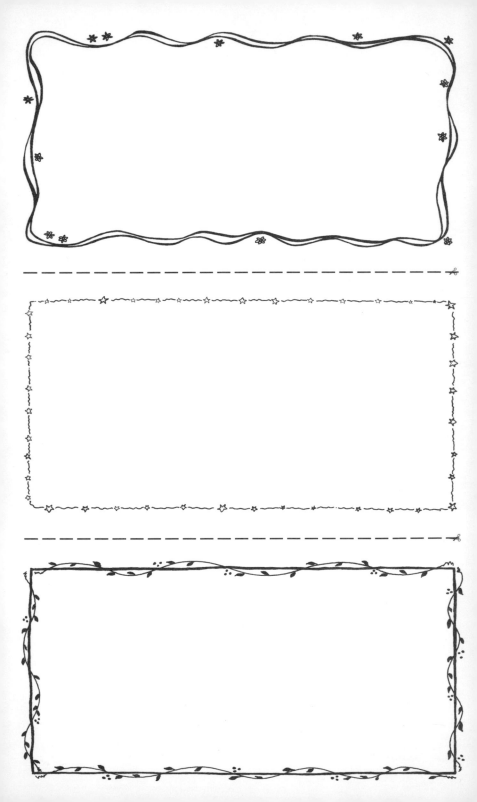

Pecan Pie Mini Muffin Mix

1 C. pecan pieces
1 1/2 C. brown sugar
2 C. all-purpose flour

Layer the ingredients in the order given into a wide-mouth 1-quart canning jar. Pack each layer into place before adding the next ingredient.

Attach a gift tag with the mixing and baking directions.

❁ *For an out of the ordinary gift, place jar mixes in a mixing bowl along with kitchen utensils, cookbooks, recipe cards, towels and pot holders.* ❁

Pecan Pie Mini Muffins

Makes 2 to 3 dozen

1 jar Pecan Pie Mini Muffin Mix
4 eggs, beaten
1 1/2 C. butter or margarine,
   melted

Preheat the oven to 350°F. In a large bowl, cream the eggs and butter. Add the Pecan Pie Mini Muffin Mix and stir until the mixture is well blended. Fill greased mini muffin pans until half full (approximately 1 tablespoon). Bake for 12 to 15 minutes. Cool in the pan on a wire rack before removing.

Pecan Pie Mini Muffins
Makes 2 to 3 dozen

1 jar Pecan Pie Mini Muffin Mix
4 eggs, beaten

1 1/2 C. butter or margarine,
melted

Preheat the oven to 350°F. In a large bowl, cream the eggs and butter. Add the Pecan Pie Mini Muffin Mix and stir until the mixture is well blended. Fill greased mini muffin pans until half full (approximately 1 tablespoon). Bake for 12 to 15 minutes. Cool in the pan on a wire rack before removing.

Pecan Pie Mini Muffins
Makes 2 to 3 dozen

1 jar Pecan Pie Mini Muffin Mix
4 eggs, beaten

1 1/2 C. butter or margarine,
melted

Preheat the oven to 350°F. In a large bowl, cream the eggs and butter. Add the Pecan Pie Mini Muffin Mix and stir until the mixture is well blended. Fill greased mini muffin pans until half full (approximately 1 tablespoon). Bake for 12 to 15 minutes. Cool in the pan on a wire rack before removing.

Pecan Pie Mini Muffins
Makes 2 to 3 dozen

1 jar Pecan Pie Mini Muffin Mix
4 eggs, beaten

1 1/2 C. butter or margarine,
melted

Preheat the oven to 350°F. In a large bowl, cream the eggs and butter. Add the Pecan Pie Mini Muffin Mix and stir until the mixture is well blended. Fill greased mini muffin pans until half full (approximately 1 tablespoon). Bake for 12 to 15 minutes. Cool in the pan on a wire rack before removing.

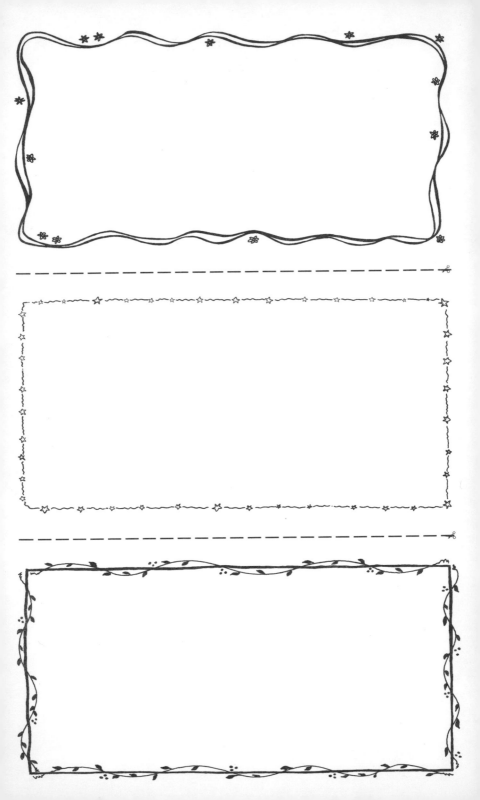

Pecan Pie Mini Muffins
Makes 2 to 3 dozen

1 jar Pecan Pie Mini Muffin Mix
4 eggs, beaten

1 1/2 C. butter or margarine,
melted

Preheat the oven to 350°F. In a large bowl, cream the eggs and butter. Add the Pecan Pie Mini Muffin Mix and stir until the mixture is well blended. Fill greased mini muffin pans until half full (approximately 1 tablespoon). Bake for 12 to 15 minutes. Cool in the pan on a wire rack before removing.

Pecan Pie Mini Muffins
Makes 2 to 3 dozen

1 jar Pecan Pie Mini Muffin Mix
4 eggs, beaten

1 1/2 C. butter or margarine,
melted

Preheat the oven to 350°F. In a large bowl, cream the eggs and butter. Add the Pecan Pie Mini Muffin Mix and stir until the mixture is well blended. Fill greased mini muffin pans until half full (approximately 1 tablespoon). Bake for 12 to 15 minutes. Cool in the pan on a wire rack before removing.

Pecan Pie Mini Muffins
Makes 2 to 3 dozen

1 jar Pecan Pie Mini Muffin Mix
4 eggs, beaten

1 1/2 C. butter or margarine,
melted

Preheat the oven to 350°F. In a large bowl, cream the eggs and butter. Add the Pecan Pie Mini Muffin Mix and stir until the mixture is well blended. Fill greased mini muffin pans until half full (approximately 1 tablespoon). Bake for 12 to 15 minutes. Cool in the pan on a wire rack before removing.

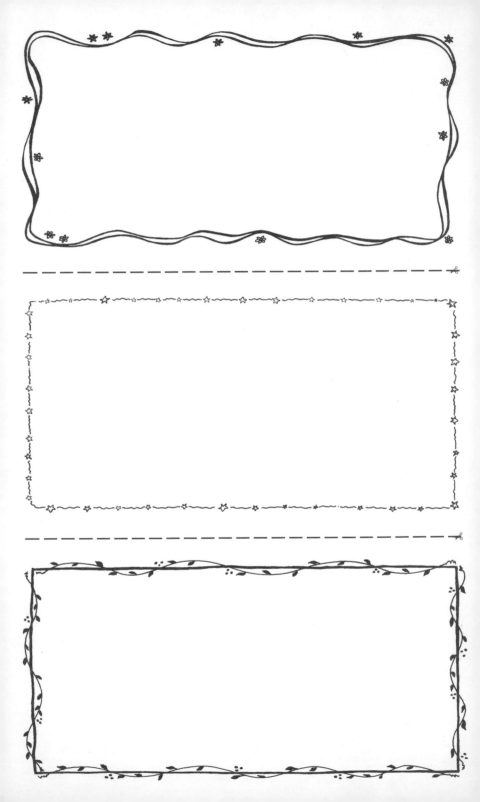

Red, White and Chocolate Cookie Mix

1/2 C. coarsely chopped
   dried cherries
1/2 C. white baking chips
1/2 C. chopped walnuts
1/2 C. brown sugar
1/2 C. sugar
1/2 C. unsweetened cocoa
1 1/2 C. all-purpose flour
1/2 tsp. baking soda
Pinch of salt

Layer the ingredients in the order given into a wide-mouth 1-quart canning jar. Pack each layer into place before adding the next ingredient.

Attach a gift tag with the mixing and baking directions.

❊ *Attach a Christmas ornament to your jar.* ❊

Red, White and Chocolate Cookies

Makes 2 to 3 dozen

1 jar Red, White and Chocolate
    Cookie Mix
2/3 C. butter or margarine,
    softened
2 eggs
1 tsp. cherry extract

Preheat the oven to 325°F. In a large bowl, cream the butter. Add the Red, White and Chocolate Cookie Mix. Stir until well blended. Beat in eggs and cherry extract. Drop by level tablespoons onto a lightly greased cookie sheet. Bake for 14 to 16 minutes. Transfer to wire racks to cool.

Red, White and Chocolate Cookies
Makes 2 to 3 dozen

1 jar Red, White and Chocolate   2 eggs
  Cookie Mix   1 tsp. cherry extract
2/3 C. butter or margarine,
  softened

    Preheat the oven to 325°F. In a large bowl, cream the butter. Add the Red, White and Chocolate Cookie Mix. Stir until well blended. Beat in eggs and cherry extract. Drop by level tablespoons onto a lightly greased cookie sheet. Bake for 14 to 16 minutes. Transfer to wire racks to cool.

Red, White and Chocolate Cookies
Makes 2 to 3 dozen

1 jar Red, White and Chocolate   2 eggs
  Cookie Mix   1 tsp. cherry extract
2/3 C. butter or margarine,
  softened

    Preheat the oven to 325°F. In a large bowl, cream the butter. Add the Red, White and Chocolate Cookie Mix. Stir until well blended. Beat in eggs and cherry extract. Drop by level tablespoons onto a lightly greased cookie sheet. Bake for 14 to 16 minutes. Transfer to wire racks to cool.

Red, White and Chocolate Cookies
Makes 2 to 3 dozen

1 jar Red, White and Chocolate   2 eggs
  Cookie Mix   1 tsp. cherry extract
2/3 C. butter or margarine,
  softened

    Preheat the oven to 325°F. In a large bowl, cream the butter. Add the Red, White and Chocolate Cookie Mix. Stir until well blended. Beat in eggs and cherry extract. Drop by level tablespoons onto a lightly greased cookie sheet. Bake for 14 to 16 minutes. Transfer to wire racks to cool.

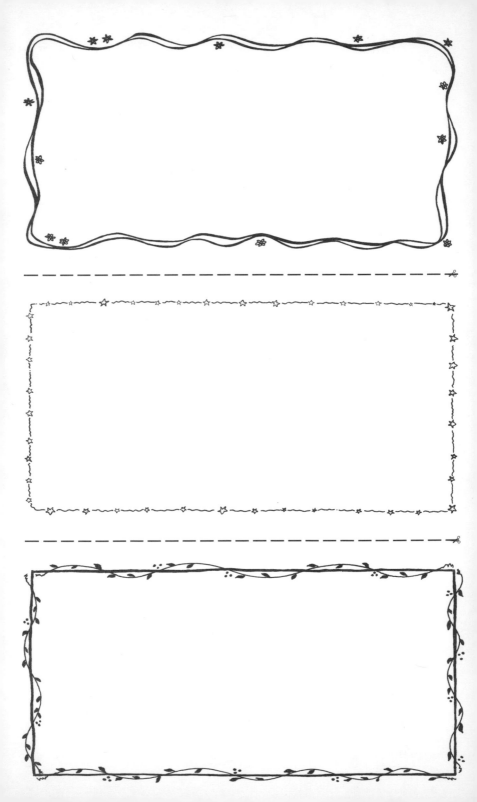

Red, White and Chocolate Cookies
Makes 2 to 3 dozen

1 jar Red, White and Chocolate
   Cookie Mix
2/3 C. butter or margarine,
   softened

2 eggs
1 tsp. cherry extract

Preheat the oven to 325°F. In a large bowl, cream the butter. Add the Red, White and Chocolate Cookie Mix. Stir until well blended. Beat in eggs and cherry extract. Drop by level tablespoons onto a lightly greased cookie sheet. Bake for 14 to 16 minutes. Transfer to wire racks to cool.

Red, White and Chocolate Cookies
Makes 2 to 3 dozen

1 jar Red, White and Chocolate
   Cookie Mix
2/3 C. butter or margarine,
   softened

2 eggs
1 tsp. cherry extract

Preheat the oven to 325°F. In a large bowl, cream the butter. Add the Red, White and Chocolate Cookie Mix. Stir until well blended. Beat in eggs and cherry extract. Drop by level tablespoons onto a lightly greased cookie sheet. Bake for 14 to 16 minutes. Transfer to wire racks to cool.

Red, White and Chocolate Cookies
Makes 2 to 3 dozen

1 jar Red, White and Chocolate
   Cookie Mix
2/3 C. butter or margarine,
   softened

2 eggs
1 tsp. cherry extract

Preheat the oven to 325°F. In a large bowl, cream the butter. Add the Red, White and Chocolate Cookie Mix. Stir until well blended. Beat in eggs and cherry extract. Drop by level tablespoons onto a lightly greased cookie sheet. Bake for 14 to 16 minutes. Transfer to wire racks to cool.

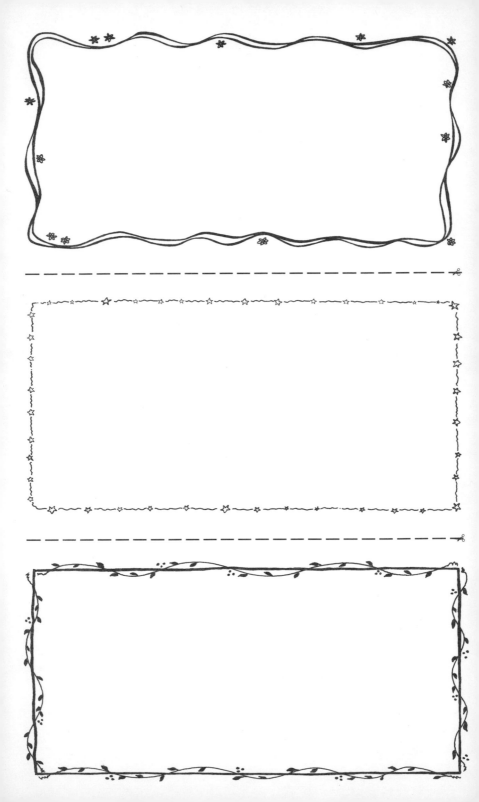

Cranberry Biscotti Mix

3/4 C. dried cranberries
3/4 C. pecans
2 C. all-purpose flour
1/2 tsp. cinnamon
2 tsp. baking powder
2/3 C. sugar

Layer the ingredients in the order given into a wide-mouth 1-quart canning jar. Pack each layer into place before adding the next ingredient.

Attach a gift tag with the mixing and baking directions.

❋ To give the jar a festive look, use an old Christmas card scene. First place lid on jar, put fabric on next, then place the card scene on top of fabric and screw on ring to secure. ❋

Cranberry Biscotti

Makes 2 1/2 to 3 dozen

1 jar Cranberry Biscotti Mix
1/3 C. butter or margarine,
  softened
2 eggs

Preheat the oven to 375°F. In a large bowl, cream butter and eggs. Add the Cranberry Biscotti Mix. Stir just until the mixture is combined. Divide the dough into 2 loaves, chilling if necessary to make dough easier to handle, and place on greased cookie sheets. Each loaf should be about 9 inches long and 2 inches wide. Bake for 25 to 30 minutes or until a toothpick inserted in the center comes out clean. Cool for 1 hour. Preheat the oven to 325°F. Cut each loaf diagonally into 1/2 inch thick slices using a serrated bread knife. Place slices on an ungreased cookie sheet. Bake for 8 minutes, then turn over and bake for 8 to 10 minutes more until dry and crisp. Transfer to wire racks to cool.

Cranberry Biscotti
Makes 2 1/2 to 3 dozen

1 jar Cranberry Biscotti Mix
2 eggs

1/3 C. butter or margarine,
softened

Preheat the oven to 375℉. In a large bowl, cream butter and eggs. Add the Cranberry Biscotti Mix. Stir just until the mixture is combined. Divide the dough into 2 loaves, chilling if necessary to make dough easier to handle, and place on greased cookie sheets. Each loaf should be about 9 inches long and 2 inches wide. Bake for 25 to 30 minutes or until a toothpick inserted in the center comes out clean. Cool for 1 hour. Preheat the oven to 325℉. Cut each loaf diagonally into 1/2 inch thick slices using a serrated bread knife. Place slices on an ungreased cookie sheet. Bake for 8 minutes, then turn over and bake for 8 to 10 minutes more until dry and crisp. Transfer to wire racks to cool.

Cranberry Biscotti
Makes 2 1/2 to 3 dozen

1 jar Cranberry Biscotti Mix
2 eggs

1/3 C. butter or margarine,
softened

Preheat the oven to 375℉. In a large bowl, cream butter and eggs. Add the Cranberry Biscotti Mix. Stir just until the mixture is combined. Divide the dough into 2 loaves, chilling if necessary to make dough easier to handle, and place on greased cookie sheets. Each loaf should be about 9 inches long and 2 inches wide. Bake for 25 to 30 minutes or until a toothpick inserted in the center comes out clean. Cool for 1 hour. Preheat the oven to 325℉. Cut each loaf diagonally into 1/2 inch thick slices using a serrated bread knife. Place slices on an ungreased cookie sheet. Bake for 8 minutes, then turn over and bake for 8 to 10 minutes more until dry and crisp. Transfer to wire racks to cool.

Cranberry Biscotti
Makes 2 1/2 to 3 dozen

1 jar Cranberry Biscotti Mix
2 eggs

1/3 C. butter or margarine,
softened

Preheat the oven to 375℉. In a large bowl, cream butter and eggs. Add the Cranberry Biscotti Mix. Stir just until the mixture is combined. Divide the dough into 2 loaves, chilling if necessary to make dough easier to handle, and place on greased cookie sheets. Each loaf should be about 9 inches long and 2 inches wide. Bake for 25 to 30 minutes or until a toothpick inserted in the center comes out clean. Cool for 1 hour. Preheat the oven to 325℉. Cut each loaf diagonally into 1/2 inch thick slices using a serrated bread knife. Place slices on an ungreased cookie sheet. Bake for 8 minutes, then turn over and bake for 8 to 10 minutes more until dry and crisp. Transfer to wire racks to cool.

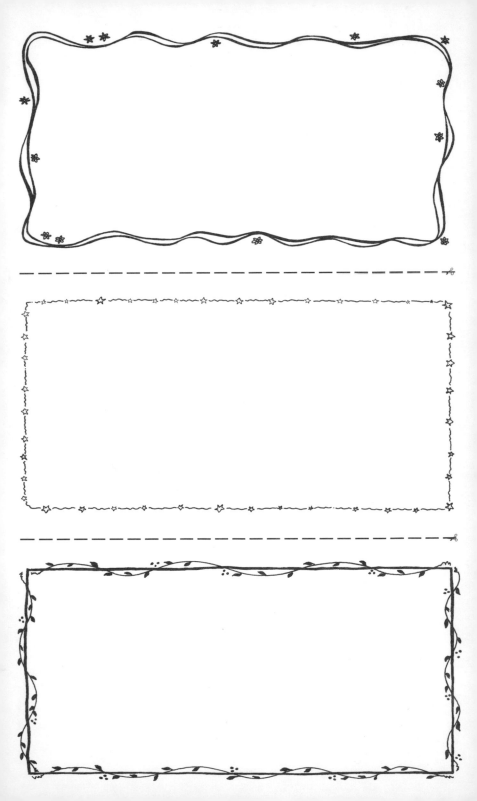

Cranberry Biscotti
Makes 2 1/2 to 3 dozen

1 jar Cranberry Biscotti Mix
2 eggs

1/3 C. butter or margarine, softened

Preheat the oven to 375°F. In a large bowl, cream butter and eggs. Add the Cranberry Biscotti Mix. Stir just until the mixture is combined. Divide the dough into 2 loaves, chilling if necessary to make dough easier to handle, and place on greased cookie sheets. Each loaf should be about 9 inches long and 2 inches wide. Bake for 25 to 30 minutes or until a toothpick inserted in the center comes out clean. Cool for 1 hour. Preheat the oven to 325°F. Cut each loaf diagonally into 1/2 inch thick slices using a serrated bread knife. Place slices on an ungreased cookie sheet. Bake for 8 minutes, then turn over and bake for 8 to 10 minutes more until dry and crisp. Transfer to wire racks to cool.

Cranberry Biscotti
Makes 2 1/2 to 3 dozen

1 jar Cranberry Biscotti Mix
2 eggs

1/3 C. butter or margarine, softened

Preheat the oven to 375°F. In a large bowl, cream butter and eggs. Add the Cranberry Biscotti Mix. Stir just until the mixture is combined. Divide the dough into 2 loaves, chilling if necessary to make dough easier to handle, and place on greased cookie sheets. Each loaf should be about 9 Inches long and 2 inches wide. Bake for 25 to 30 minutes or until a toothpick inserted in the center comes out clean. Cool for 1 hour. Preheat the oven to 325°F. Cut each loaf diagonally into 1/2 inch thick slices using a serrated bread knife. Place slices on an ungreased cookie sheet. Bake for 8 minutes, then turn over and bake for 8 to 10 minutes more until dry and crisp. Transfer to wire racks to cool.

Cranberry Biscotti
Makes 2 1/2 to 3 dozen

1 jar Cranberry Biscotti Mix
2 eggs

1/3 C. butter or margarine, softened

Preheat the oven to 375°F. In a large bowl, cream butter and eggs. Add the Cranberry Biscotti Mix. Stir just until the mixture is combined. Divide the dough into 2 loaves, chilling if necessary to make dough easier to handle, and place on greased cookie sheets. Each loaf should be about 9 inches long and 2 inches wide. Bake for 25 to 30 minutes or until a toothpick inserted in the center comes out clean. Cool for 1 hour. Preheat the oven to 325°F. Cut each loaf diagonally into 1/2 inch thick slices using a serrated bread knife. Place slices on an ungreased cookie sheet. Bake for 8 minutes, then turn over and bake for 8 to 10 minutes more until dry and crisp. Transfer to wire racks to cool.

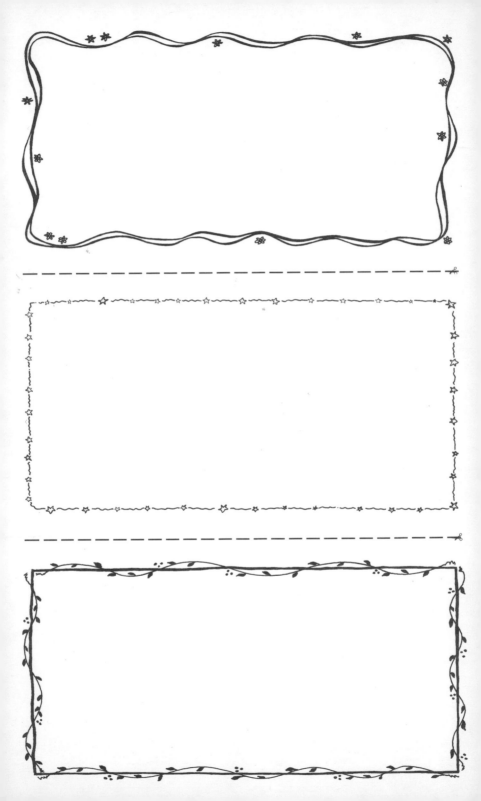

Holiday M&M Oatmeal Bar Mix

1/2 C. old-fashioned oats
1/2 C. mini M&M's
1/2 C. light brown sugar
1 C. biscuit and baking mix
1/2 C. dark brown sugar
1 C. biscuit and baking mix

Layer the ingredients in the order given into a wide-mouth 1-quart canning jar. Pack each layer into place before adding the next ingredient.

Attach a gift tag with the mixing and baking directions.

❋ Small appliques or embroidery can be added to the center of a fabric cover to further personalize the gift. ❋

Holiday M&M Oatmeal Bars

Makes 16 bars

1 jar Holiday M&M Oatmeal
   Bar Mix
1/2 C. butter or margarine,
   melted
1 egg
1 tsp. vanilla

Preheat the oven to 350°F. In a large bowl, cream the butter, egg and vanilla. Add the Holiday M&M Oatmeal Bar Mix. Stir until the mixture is well blended. Press into a greased 8-inch square baking pan. Bake for 18 to 22 minutes or until bars are a light golden brown and center is almost set. Cool before cutting.

Holiday M&M Oatmeal Bars
Makes 16 bars

1 jar Holiday M&M Oatmeal
  Bar Mix
1/2 C. butter or margarine,
  melted

1 egg
1 tsp. vanilla

Preheat the oven to 350°F. In a large bowl, cream the butter, egg and vanilla. Add the Holiday M&M Oatmeal Bar Mix. Stir until the mixture is well blended. Press into a greased 8-inch square baking pan. Bake for 18 to 22 minutes or until bars are a light golden brown and center is almost set. Cool before cutting.

Holiday M&M Oatmeal Bars
Makes 16 bars

1 jar Holiday M&M Oatmeal
  Bar Mix
1/2 C. butter or margarine,
  melted

1 egg
1 tsp. vanilla

Preheat the oven to 350°F. In a large bowl, cream the butter, egg and vanilla. Add the Holiday M&M Oatmeal Bar Mix. Stir until the mixture is well blended. Press into a greased 8-inch square baking pan. Bake for 18 to 22 minutes or until bars are a light golden brown and center is almost set. Cool before cutting.

White Christmas Cherry Bar Mix

1/4 C. white chocolate or
   vanilla chips
1/2 C. chopped pecans, toasted
   and cooled completely*
1/2 C. sweetened dried cherries
   or cranberries
1/2 C. light brown sugar
1 C. biscuit and baking mix
1/2 C. dark brown sugar
1 C. biscuit and baking mix

Layer the ingredients in the order given into a wide-mouth 1-quart canning jar. Pack each layer into place before adding the next ingredient.

Attach a gift tag with the mixing and baking directions.

*To toast pecans, place nuts in a single layer on a baking sheet. Bake at 350°F for approximately 10 minutes or until nuts are golden brown.

White Christmas Cherry Bars

Makes 16 bars

1 jar White Christmas Cherry
   Bar Mix
1/2 C. butter or margarine,
   melted
1 egg
1 tsp. vanilla

Preheat the oven to 350°F. In a large bowl, cream butter, egg and vanilla. Add the White Christmas Cherry Bar Mix. Stir until the mixture is well blended. Press into a greased 8-inch square baking pan. Bake for 20 to 22 minutes or until bars are golden brown and center is almost set. Cool before cutting.

White Christmas Cherry Bars
Makes 16 bars

1 jar White Christmas Cherry
  Bar Mix
1/2 C. butter or margarine, melted

1 egg
1 tsp. vanilla

Preheat the oven to 350°F. In a large bowl, cream butter, egg and vanilla. Add the White Christmas Cherry Bar Mix. Stir until the mixture is well blended. Press into a greased 8-inch square baking pan. Bake for 20 to 22 minutes or until bars are golden brown and center is almost set. Cool before cutting.

White Christmas Cherry Bars
Makes 16 bars

1 jar White Christmas Cherry
  Bar Mix
1/2 C. butter or margarine, melted

1 egg
1 tsp. vanilla

Preheat the oven to 350°F. In a large bowl, cream butter, egg and vanilla. Add the White Christmas Cherry Bar Mix. Stir until the mixture is well blended. Press into a greased 8-inch square baking pan. Bake for 20 to 22 minutes or until bars are golden brown and center is almost set. Cool before cutting.

White Christmas Cherry Bars
Makes 16 bars

1 jar White Christmas Cherry
  Bar Mix
1/2 C. butter or margarine, melted

1 egg
1 tsp. vanilla

Preheat the oven to 350°F. In a large bowl, cream butter, egg and vanilla. Add the White Christmas Cherry Bar Mix. Stir until the mixture is well blended. Press into a greased 8-inch square baking pan. Bake for 20 to 22 minutes or until bars are golden brown and center is almost set. Cool before cutting.

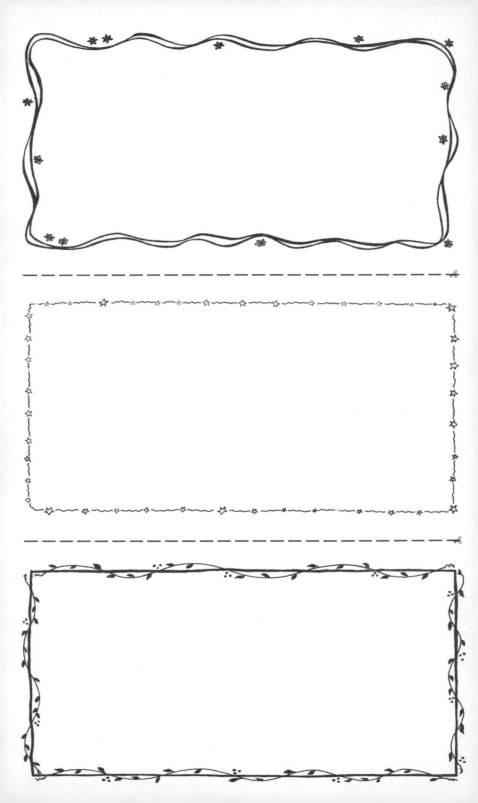

White Christmas Cherry Bars
Makes 16 bars

1 jar White Christmas Cherry
  Bar Mix
1/2 C. butter or margarine, melted

1 egg
1 tsp. vanilla

Preheat the oven to 350°F. In a large bowl, cream butter, egg and vanilla. Add the White Christmas Cherry Bar Mix. Stir until the mixture is well blended. Press into a greased 8-inch square baking pan. Bake for 20 to 22 minutes or until bars are golden brown and center is almost set. Cool before cutting.

White Christmas Cherry Bars
Makes 16 bars

1 jar White Christmas Cherry
  Bar Mix
1/2 C. butter or margarine, melted

1 egg
1 tsp. vanilla

Preheat the oven to 350°F. In a large bowl, cream butter, egg and vanilla. Add the White Christmas Cherry Bar Mix. Stir until the mixture is well blended. Press into a greased 8-inch square baking pan. Bake for 20 to 22 minutes or until bars are golden brown and center is almost set. Cool before cutting.

White Christmas Cherry Bars
Makes 16 bars

1 jar White Christmas Cherry
  Bar Mix
1/2 C. butter or margarine, melted

1 egg
1 tsp. vanilla

Preheat the oven to 350°F. In a large bowl, cream butter, egg and vanilla. Add the White Christmas Cherry Bar Mix. Stir until the mixture is well blended. Press into a greased 8-inch square baking pan. Bake for 20 to 22 minutes or until bars are golden brown and center is almost set. Cool before cutting.

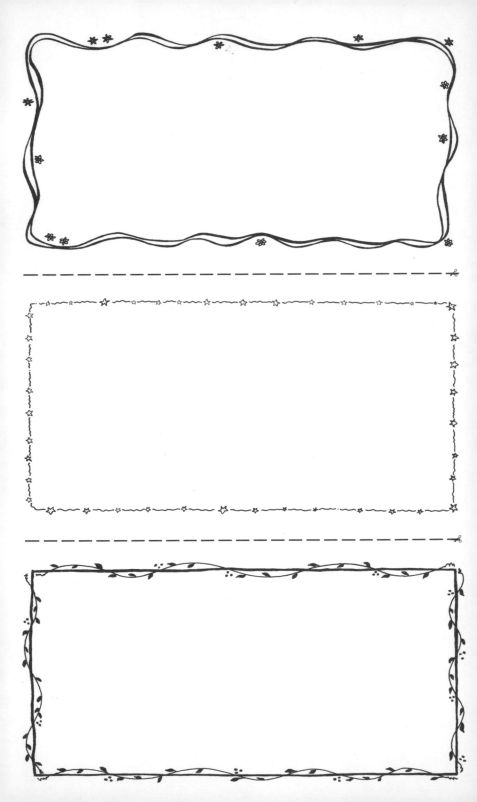

Holiday Hustle-Bustle Butterscotch-Oatmeal Cookie Mix

1/2 C. butterscotch chips
1/2 C. dark brown sugar
1 C. old-fashioned oats
1 C. biscuit and baking mix
1/2 C. light brown sugar
1 C. biscuit and baking mix

Layer the ingredients in the order given into a wide-mouth 1-quart canning jar. Pack each layer into place before adding the next ingredient.

Attach a gift tag with the mixing and baking directions.

❁ *To make a gift in a jar fancier, decorate it with a doily and ribbon.* ❁

Holiday Hustle-Bustle Butterscotch-Oatmeal Cookies

1 jar Holiday Hustle-Bustle
   Butterscotch-Oatmeal
   Cookie Mix
1/2 C. butter or margarine,
   melted
1 egg
1 tsp. vanilla

    Preheat the oven to 375°F. In a medium bowl, cream the butter, egg and vanilla. Add the Holiday Hustle-Bustle Butterscotch-Oatmeal Cookie Mix and stir until well blended. Shape into 1-inch balls. Place on a greased baking sheet. Bake for 10 to 12 minutes or until cookies are a light golden brown. Transfer to wire racks to cool.

Holiday Hustle-Bustle Butterscotch-Oatmeal Cookies

1 jar Holiday Hustle-Bustle
  Butterscotch-Oatmeal Cookie Mix
1 tsp. vanilla

1 egg
1/2 C. butter or
  margarine, melted

Preheat the oven to 375°F. In a medium bowl, cream the butter, egg and vanilla. Add the Holiday Hustle-Bustle Butterscotch-Oatmeal Cookie Mix and stir until well blended. Shape into 1-inch balls. Place on a greased baking sheet. Bake for 10 to 12 minutes or until cookies are a light golden brown. Transfer to wire racks to cool.

Holiday Hustle-Bustle Butterscotch-Oatmeal Cookies

1 jar Holiday Hustle-Bustle
  Butterscotch-Oatmeal Cookie Mix
1 tsp. vanilla

1 egg
1/2 C. butter or
  margarine, melted

Preheat the oven to 375°F. In a medium bowl, cream the butter, egg and vanilla. Add the Holiday Hustle-Bustle Butterscotch-Oatmeal Cookie Mix and stir until well blended. Shape into 1-inch balls. Place on a greased baking sheet. Bake for 10 to 12 minutes or until cookies are a light golden brown. Transfer to wire racks to cool.

Holiday Hustle-Bustle Butterscotch-Oatmeal Cookies

1 jar Holiday Hustle-Bustle
  Butterscotch-Oatmeal Cookie Mix
1 tsp. vanilla

1 egg
1/2 C. butter or
  margarine, melted

Preheat the oven to 375°F. In a medium bowl, cream the butter, egg and vanilla. Add the Holiday Hustle-Bustle Butterscotch-Oatmeal Cookie Mix and stir until well blended. Shape into 1-inch balls. Place on a greased baking sheet. Bake for 10 to 12 minutes or until cookies are a light golden brown. Transfer to wire racks to cool.

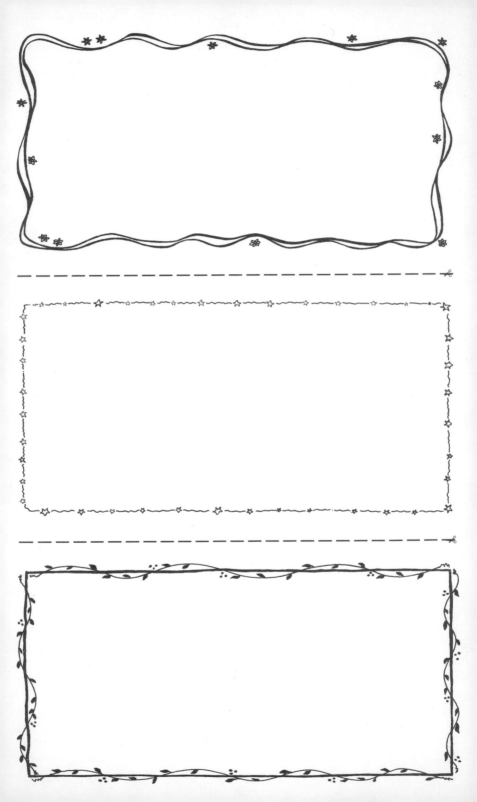

Holiday Hustle-Bustle Butterscotch-Oatmeal Cookies

1 jar Holiday Hustle-Bustle
  Butterscotch-Oatmeal Cookie Mix
1 tsp. vanilla

1 egg
1/2 C. butter or
  margarine, melted

Preheat the oven to 375°F. In a medium bowl, cream the butter, egg and vanilla. Add the Holiday Hustle-Bustle Butterscotch-Oatmeal Cookie Mix and stir until well blended. Shape into 1-inch balls. Place on a greased baking sheet. Bake for 10 to 12 minutes or until cookies are a light golden brown. Transfer to wire racks to cool.

Holiday Hustle-Bustle Butterscotch-Oatmeal Cookies

1 jar Holiday Hustle-Bustle
  Butterscotch-Oatmeal Cookie Mix
1 tsp. vanilla

1 egg
1/2 C. butter or
  margarine, melted

Preheat the oven to 375°F. In a medium bowl, cream the butter, egg and vanilla. Add the Holiday Hustle-Bustle Butterscotch-Oatmeal Cookie Mix and stir until well blended. Shape into 1-inch balls. Place on a greased baking sheet. Bake for 10 to 12 minutes or until cookies are a light golden brown. Transfer to wire racks to cool.

Holiday Hustle-Bustle Butterscotch-Oatmeal Cookies

1 jar Holiday Hustle-Bustle
  Butterscotch-Oatmeal Cookie Mix
1 tsp. vanilla

1 egg
1/2 C. butter or
  margarine, melted

Preheat the oven to 375°F. In a medium bowl, cream the butter, egg and vanilla. Add the Holiday Hustle-Bustle Butterscotch-Oatmeal Cookie Mix and stir until well blended. Shape into 1-inch balls. Place on a greased baking sheet. Bake for 10 to 12 minutes or until cookies are a light golden brown. Transfer to wire racks to cool.

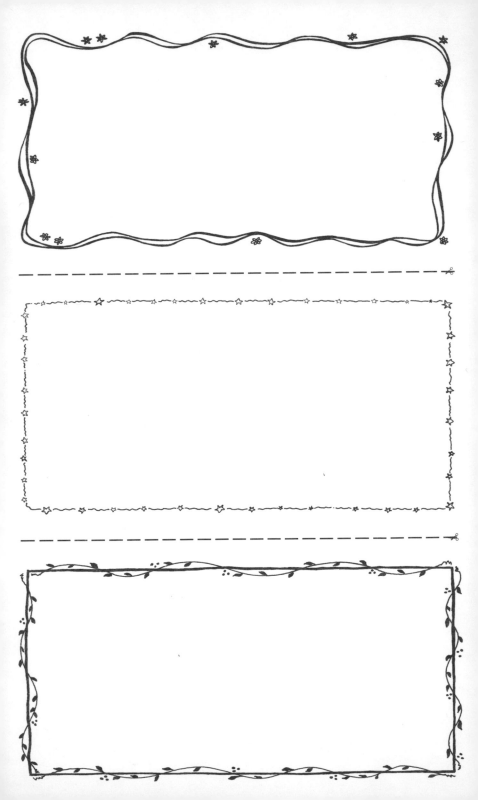

Crunchy Toffee Cookie Mix

2/3 C. toffee chips
1/2 C. chopped pecans,
    toasted and cooled
    completely*
1/2 C. dark brown sugar
1 C. biscuit and baking mix
1/2 C. light brown sugar
1 C. biscuit and baking mix

Layer the ingredients in the order given into a wide-mouth 1-quart canning jar. Pack each layer into place before adding the next ingredient.

Attach a gift tag with the mixing and baking directions.

*To toast pecans, place nuts in a single layer on a baking sheet. Bake at 350°F for approximately 10 minutes or until nuts are golden brown.

Crunchy Toffee Cookies

1 jar Crunchy Toffee Cookie Mix
1/2 C. butter or margarine,
   melted
1 egg
1 tsp. vanilla

Preheat the oven to 375°F. In a medium bowl, cream the butter, egg and vanilla. Add the Crunchy Toffee Cookie Mix and stir until well blended. Shape into 1-inch balls. Place on a greased baking sheet. Bake for 10 to 12 minutes or until cookies are a light golden brown. Transfer to wire racks to cool.

Crunchy Toffee Cookies

1 jar Crunchy Toffee Cookie Mix
1/2 C. butter or margarine,
   melted

1 egg
1 tsp. vanilla

    Preheat the oven to 375°F. In a medium bowl, cream the butter, egg and vanilla. Add the Crunchy Toffee Cookie Mix and stir until well blended. Shape into 1-inch balls. Place on a greased baking sheet. Bake for 10 to 12 minutes or until cookies are a light golden brown. Transfer to wire racks to cool.

Crunchy Toffee Cookies

1 jar Crunchy Toffee Cookie Mix
1/2 C. butter or margarine,
   melted

1 egg
1 tsp. vanilla

    Preheat the oven to 375°F. In a medium bowl, cream the butter, egg and vanilla. Add the Crunchy Toffee Cookie Mix and stir until well blended. Shape into 1-inch balls. Place on a greased baking sheet. Bake for 10 to 12 minutes or until cookies are a light golden brown. Transfer to wire racks to cool.

Crunchy Toffee Cookies

1 jar Crunchy Toffee Cookie Mix
1/2 C. butter or margarine,
   melted

1 egg
1 tsp. vanilla

    Preheat the oven to 375°F. In a medium bowl, cream the butter, egg and vanilla. Add the Crunchy Toffee Cookie Mix and stir until well blended. Shape into 1-inch balls. Place on a greased baking sheet. Bake for 10 to 12 minutes or until cookies are a light golden brown. Transfer to wire racks to cool.

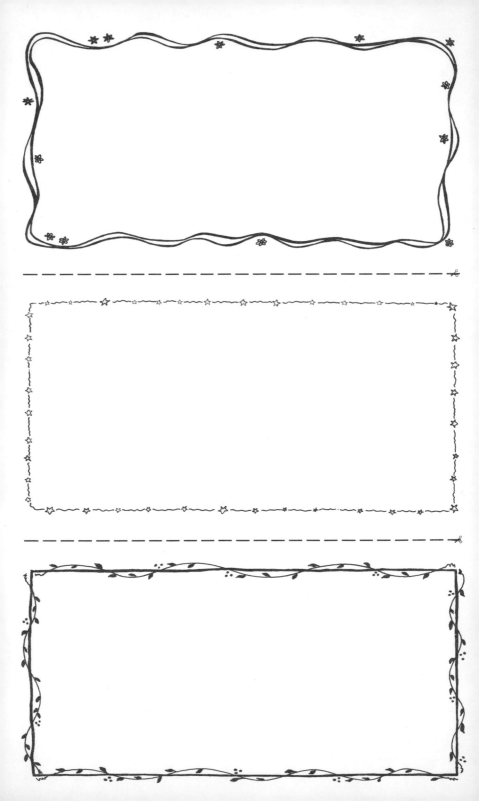

Crunchy Toffee Cookies

1 jar Crunchy Toffee Cookie Mix   1 egg
1/2 C. butter or margarine,   1 tsp. vanilla
   melted

      Preheat the oven to 375°F. In a medium bowl, cream the butter, egg and vanilla. Add the Crunchy Toffee Cookie Mix and stir until well blended. Shape into 1-inch balls. Place on a greased baking sheet. Bake for 10 to 12 minutes or until cookies are a light golden brown. Transfer to wire racks to cool.

Crunchy Toffee Cookies

1 jar Crunchy Toffee Cookie Mix   1 egg
1/2 C. butter or margarine,   1 tsp. vanilla
   melted

      Preheat the oven to 375°F. In a medium bowl, cream the butter, egg and vanilla. Add the Crunchy Toffee Cookie Mix and stir until well blended. Shape into 1-inch balls. Place on a greased baking sheet. Bake for 10 to 12 minutes or until cookies are a light golden brown. Transfer to wire racks to cool.

Crunchy Toffee Cookies

1 jar Crunchy Toffee Cookie Mix   1 egg
1/2 C. butter or margarine,   1 tsp. vanilla
   melted

      Preheat the oven to 375°F. In a medium bowl, cream the butter, egg and vanilla. Add the Crunchy Toffee Cookie Mix and stir until well blended. Shape into 1-inch balls. Place on a greased baking sheet. Bake for 10 to 12 minutes or until cookies are a light golden brown. Transfer to wire racks to cool.

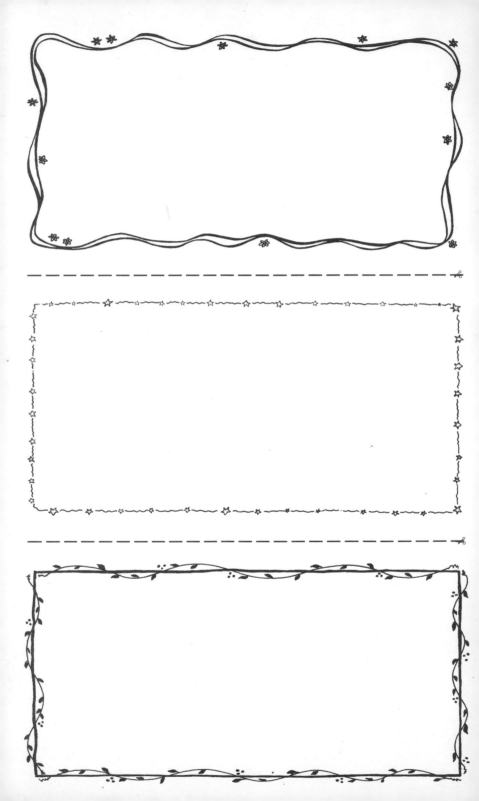